# Contents

# Contents

Contents

# 1. Introduction

Z-Wave is an international standard for wireless communication in intelligent homes. It interconnects different devices such as lighting, heating climate control, media and entertainment, safety installations and security systems. The interconnection of all these systems creates a smart home where different devices from different vendors work together to increase safety security convenience and life quality of the people living in this environment. Above and beyond this, a smart home helps to save energy and to protect human life and environment.

The key to smart home is the interconnection of different devices in the home and the ability to control all of them through a single user interface that may be a web browser, a wall touch panel, a dedicated remote control or a mobile phone.

The interconnection of devices in a residential home requires a common communication media. There are three different approaches:

- Wired solutions require dedicated cables that need to be installed during the building or a major renovation of a home. Wired solutions such as BACNet(BACnet is a protocol, it can run on different media types), certain versions of LON or KNX resp. Instabus in Europe are typically expensive and therefore only used in commercial installations and very few high-end residential homes.

- Powerline communication is using the 110 V or 230 V mains power installation as communication media. Certain standards such as HomeplugAV become more common but rather used as a replacement for Ethernet technology applied for media distributions such as TV, Video and Audio.

- Wireless solutions show the biggest growth in the market since they are both reliable and affordable and can be applied in homes without major refurbishments. Additionally, certain technologies such as intelligent door locks or sensors can hardly be installed with wires because they are on moving devices such as doors or they shall be applied on places where no wires are available.

It is for these reasons this paper focusses on wireless technologies as the technology of choice for interconnecting devices in a smart home.

## 1.1. What is a smart home

Smart Homes is a term often used along with the more descriptive term home automation. Wikipedia defines home automation as:

" Home automation is the residential extension of "building automation". It is automation of the home, housework or household activity. Home automation may include centralized control of lighting, HVAC (heating, ventilation and air conditioning), appliances, and other systems, to provide improved convenience, comfort, energy efficiency and security. Home automation for the elderly and disabled can provide increased quality of life for persons who might otherwise require caregivers or institutional care. A home automation system integrates electrical devices in a house with each other. The techniques employed in home automation include those in building automation as well as the control of domestic activities, such as home entertainment systems, houseplant and yard watering, pet feeding, changing the ambiance "scenes" for different events (such as dinners or parties), and the use of domestic robots. Devices may be connected through a computer network to allow control by a personal computer, and may allow remote access from the internet. Through the integration of information technologies with the home environment, systems and appliances are able to communicate in an integrated manner which results in convenience, energy efficiency, and safety benefits. " [SmartHome]

## 1. Introduction

The definition is accurate but not very insightful. Lets start with the obvious: In the good old time, the controlling part and the controlled part of a function in the home were located in the same device. A candle was lit right at the candle and the light came right from the candle. A door knocker was operated right at the device and generated noise right at the same device.

The advent of electricity in the last 100 years has partly changed this reality. The electronic door bell is operated at the door by pressing a button and the more or less ugly sound of the bell comes from a 'bell' connected with the door button by an electrical circuit. The electrical light is typically controlled by a wall switch that is not longer located right next to the light bulb but on a convenient location next to the door where the resident can easily access it when entering the room. The wall switch is again connected to the light bulbs via an electrical circuit.

Other examples are the control of the window blinds, the wall thermostats to control the heat in the room or a simple remote control to turn on and off devices that are inconvenient to access directly. The home is mixed with various devices that are still controlled and operated right at the devices. Examples of such devices include dishwasher, washing machine, dryer or electric stove. TVs moved out of this category about 40 years ago when the infrared remote control became the standard device to control them.

Image1.1 shows the situation in a traditional home of the early twenty-first century reflecting the different ways to control devices in the home. The Smart Home or home automation change this situation in multiple ways.

10

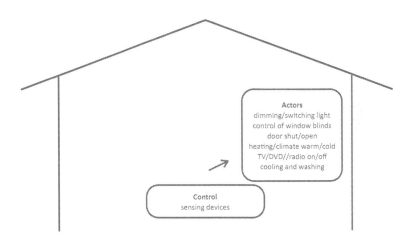

Figure 1.1.: Traditional Home of the late Nineties of the 20th century

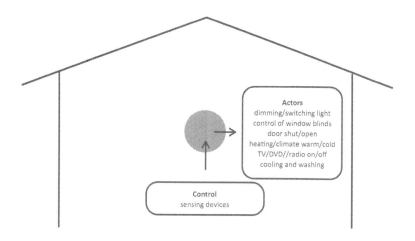

Figure 1.2.: First step into smart home

First of all, the control of various devices is unified. The light switch may not longer only control a light but as well other functions of the room. A remote control is not longer dedicated to one single device but to multiple entertainment devices and home functions such as light or climate control.

Image1.2 demonstrates this first step into smart home.

This first step offers a first simplification of usage and control to the resident. It unifies the operations concept and allows using single point of controls that are more convenient to use. Good examples of such single point of controls are mobile phones that have become more and more the central point of control to various functions and services in people's lives.

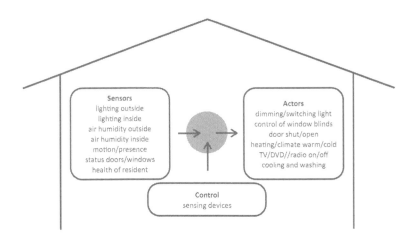

Figure 1.3.: Second step into smart home

The second function of a smart home is the use of sensors that give further information about the status of the home and actions to be undertaken to improve the convenience and security of the resident. By no means this is a new concept. Wall thermostats have a temperature sensor inside that is used to control the heating in the room and the smoke detector is also a sensor as such. The concept of a smart home brings the idea of sensor controlling the room to a new level. Motion detectors control the light if people are in a room or turn down or even off the heating when people have left the room. Air quality sensors control windows and ventilation to guarantee enough oxygen in the room when occupied.

This second function is represented by Image1.3.

13

## 1. Introduction

Last but not least the core function of a smart home is the automation. An intelligent entity interconnects the different information given either by sensors or by the residents interactions - e.g. operating a button to create intelligent control of the different functions of the home. It is connecting different functions, already unified in their manual operation by the first aspect of smart home into a self-thinking entity that makes sure that the home is executing functions automatically and independent of dedicated user interaction.

A good example is the control of a roof window. In winter time, the windows shall be closed with shutters during the night to preserve as much energy as possible. During the day, the window blinds may go up and at noon, if the outside temperature is sensed to be high enough, the windows open automatically to bring fresh air into the building. A rain and a wind sensor provide information to keep the window closed during heavy wind or rain. In summer time, the automation may be different. Now the window shall be closed during daytime with blinds down to prevent overheating and it shall open up at night to get fresh air into the building. Of course, rain and wind protection are provided as well. If the automation control knows that the resident is not in the building, the windows may be closed 24 hours for security reason. Beside the control of the home the interconnected system of sensors and acting devices - also referred to as actuators - can provide information about certain measurement values to status of the home and the resident. This may help to further optimize the functions of the home but also inform the user about the safety and security and help to conserve energy when possible.

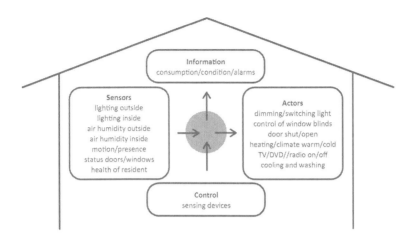

Figure 1.4.: Final step into smart home

Image1.4 shows this final step into smart home. The characteristics of a smart home can be defined as

> " **Different unified user interfaces control different actions in the home using the users interaction, sensor data and intelligent decisions made by the control itself. The same time the smart home provides useful information for the resident to help to make smarter decisions such as conserving energy.** "

There is no clear borderline when a home starts to become a Smart Home. When wired communication technologies are used, the homebuilder has to decide prior to the construction what kind of intelligent or non-intelligent functions he wants to apply in the building. Particularly, the use of wireless technology allow however to step by step introduce new functions and make the living or working environment more and more intelligent.

## 1.2. Smart Home Definitions

There are some common characteristics and basic language used in every smart home environment.

- **Sensor:** A sensor is a device that generates information and delivers it to other devices in the network using a communication network. Examples of such sensors are the temperature sensor in the room thermostat, motion detectors, door sensors or smoke detectors.

- **Controllers:** Controllers are devices that control other devices using the communication network between them. They typically provide a user interface. Examples of controllers are remote controls, keypads or wall switches.

- **Actors:** Actors - also referred to as actuators - are devices that perform an action. They switch, dim, turn on or off, wind up, shut down etc. Examples of actors are window motors, light switches, light dimmers, electronic door locks.

- **Control Network:** The network is a the communication medium that interconnects actors, controllers and sensors.

- **Gateways:** Gateways interconnect the home communication network to other communication networks such as TCP/IP (Transmission Control Protocol/Internet Protocol) based Internet or the cell phone network.

The intelligence of the home control network may reside in one single device - typically the gateway because it needs higher computing power anyway - or may be distributed amongst various devices.

Certain devices may also mix different functions in one single hardware device. Multiple sensors - e.g. temperature or humidity are very common. Another example of such a hybrid device is a room thermostat that typically combines a temperature sensor with a user interface to set the desired temperature in the room.

## 1.3. General Layer Model of wireless communication network

Wireless communication systems are complex and consist of a huge number of functions. To structure all these functions communication engineers cluster them into a layer stack or protocol stack. The idea of the layer stack is that one layer is using the services of the underlying layer and is providing a function to the layer above. There functions are well defined so that it is - at least in theory - possible to replace one implementation of a layer by another different implementation without changing the rest of the stack. Each layer has its defined functions to be performed and these functions

## 1. Introduction

define the services one layer is offering to the upper layer. For communication networks in smart homes a four layer structure is very usable:

1. **Radio Layer:** This layer defines the way a signal is exchanged between a transmitter and a receiver. This includes issues like frequency, encoding, hardware access, etc. The service the radio layer is providing is the transport of different bits and bytes from one device to another device.

2. **Network Layer:** This layer makes sure that data are transmitted secured and reliable from the source to the destination. In a wireless radio network this may require to use certain devices as wireless repeaters. The functions of the network layer include the organisation of the network (who is in who is out), addressing, routing, encryption, data retransmission and data.

3. **Application Layer:** The application layer defines the meaning of the data transmitted by the network layer and subsequently the radio layer. The network layer only knows bytes. The application layer defines the meaning of the bytes and how they form a command. Application layer defines the format of metering and measuring values, the different commands used to perform certain actions.

4. **User interface:** The user interface layer acts as interface to the user itself. It defines how certain functions of the network and certain status information are presented on different user interfaces such as cell phone or

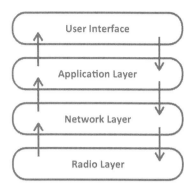

Figure 1.5.: Generic four layers of a wireless communication
network

tablet screen or even on a wall switch. User interface
defines things like meanings of icons, LED blinking se-
quences, number and speed of needed button presses
etc.

This four layer structure is shown in Figure 1.5. This
book will organize the description of the Z-Wave wireless
communication protocol using this layer model.

## 1.4. Requirements of a wireless system for home control

The communication network of a smart home needs to meet a set of important requirements. Since wireless technologies are the clear winning choice compared with wire based technology, the following comparison will focus on wireless technologies only.

Requirements are:

1. Reliability of the communication: It is essential for important functions such as door locks, alarm and heating to be reliable. In order to ensure this reliability it is essential that all messages will reach their destination and are confirmed by the receiving device back to the transmitter. This two-way, every message sent is confirmed or acknowledged back to the transmitter, is what defines reliable communication. Not all wireless network technologies comply to this requirement.

2. Security of communication: It must be guaranteed that an unauthorized third party cannot on purpose or accidentally intercept or interfere with the communication of the communication system. Typically encoding technologies and handshake mechanisms ensure this.

3. Low power radio emission: It is essential for health and safety as well as for interference with other wireless devices such as phones, radios and TVs that the wireless technology for home automation is as low

power as possible. This is also helpful in achieving extended battery life for battery powered devices.

4. Simple usage: Home Automation shall make the life of the user easier and not more complicated.

5. Adequate price: That is an obvious point to ensure broad acceptance of the technology.

6. Protection of investment: Home automation solutions are typically installed during the construction of new buildings or renovation and need to comply with typical product life cycles of home installation equipment. It is important to make sure, that the user can replace devices or extend their systems even after years and do not run into compatibility issues.

7. Interoperability: Home Automation functions such as heating, lighting or window control are implemented with products from different vendors each with expertise in their respective areas. It is not acceptable to be forced to stick with one vendor and buy - as an example - heating technology from a vendor with core competence in lighting just to enable interoperability of all system devices. Each installed wireless technology has to be used independent from several manufacturers. Cross vendor interoperability is ensured by strong technology standards and product certification programs. Good examples of interoperability are WiFi, Bluetooth and Z-Wave.

# 1.5. Alternatives for wireless home control networks

On the market there are various wireless communication technologies for smart homes that comply more or less with the requirements just outlined.

## 1.5.1. Analogue Control using 27 MHz or 433 MHz frequency band

Analogue wireless systems are typically available from no-name vendors and have a remarkably low price. The strong focus on entry level performance and the price typically results in low manufacturing quality and very poor security. Because the frequency is used is often shared with baby monitor radios or CB transceivers, interference is common and the behavior of this equipment becomes unpredictable. Because of these limitations analogue wireless systems are not widely used for more serious installations in homes. They are more and more replaced by digital systems that are more reliable and have higher levels of performance and flexibility.

1. **Reliability of communication:** no

2. **Security of communication:** no

3. **Low radio emission:** yes

4. **Simple usage:** yes

5. **Low price:** yes

6. **Protection of investment:** no

7. **Interoperability:** no

## 1.5.2. Proprietary digital protocols from different vendors

Multiple manufacturers have developed their own proprietary digital solution for wireless control and some of them offer a variety of different products. Some of these protocols have implemented two-way. reliable communication with full acknowledge of transmission.

By far the biggest disadvantage of these solutions is the fact that the communication technology used is proprietary or private to one or a very small number of vendors. This does not pose a problem for a simple solution but often prevents the implementation of a complete automation or control solution. Not only will types of products be limited having one vendor it bears a great risk for long-term availability of products. It is not uncommon to see vendors change protocols and make the former products obsolete. Nevertheless proprietary technologies play their role in the market mainly because of substantial marketing efforts from the companies owning these technologies and their one-stop simplicity in purchasing.

1. **Reliability of communication:** partly

2. **Security of communication:** partly

3. **Low radio emission:** yes

4. **Simple usage:** yes

5. **Low price:** yes

6. **Protection of investment:** no

7. **Interoperability:** no

## 1.5.3. Wifi or WLAN

Wireless LAN (WLAN) is most likely the technology with the highest market penetration. Virtually all notebooks, netbooks, all tablet PCs, almost all smart phones have WLAN interface built in. This bears the obvious question what smart homes are not utilizing WLAN as the standard communication network. Actually there are three reasons:

(1) WLAN is designed for transmitting large amount of data and therefore is using a lot of energy for transmissions and reception. The clear focus on speed, high security and large transmission ratio comes at a big price: WLAN takes way too much energy for a home control network that is at least partly built on battery powered devices or even devices using energy harvesting. WLAN therefore can be used in parts of the smart home where devices are mains powered but it cannot cover the whole range of applications. The interconnection of smart home devices to cell phones or tablets is typically done using WLAN to a gateway device and then some other lower speed, lower power technology is used from the gateway to the end devices, the sensors and actuators. There are various attempts to decrease the power consumption of WLAN but none of them comes nearly to a level where battery operated devices can be used at a reasonable battery life time.

(2) WLAN is using the 2.4 GHz and 5 GHz radio spectrum and that spectrum or band is getting more and more saturated. At the moment this is not yet a big problem in typical residential homes but more and more high energy WLAN transmitters are getting deployed usually for digital media streaming, Netflicks, WirelessHD and the like hence creating a big future risk for any technology that shares this spectrum. Exhibitors at trade shows such as CES, Cebit or Light + Building already know that a certain amount of active WLAN devices in a room will certainly shut down all WLAN communication.

(3) WLAN only specifies the radio layer and the network layer. So far there is no generally accepted application layer specification for smart homes based on WLAN. This means that different devices using WLAN can work in one single network but cannot interoperate with each other. The Internet Engineering Task Force (IETF) as standardization body of the Internet application layers is working on this issue but so far there is no widely accepted standard available. The only currently available link between Internet/WLAN technology and smart home is the so called 6LoPAN specification [6LoPAN]. 6LoPAn defines how to map an IP address to the addresses used in the internet and to wireless technologies typically used in smart homes. The aim is to create the internet of things where each and every device in the home has its own IP address and is reachable from the internet. The reader may decide whether this is a desirable solution from the security and privacy point of view.

1. **Reliability of communication:** mainly yes

2. **Security of communication:** yes

3. **Low radio emission:** no

4. **Simple usage:** yes

5. **Low price:** yes

6. **Protection of investment:** no proprietary application layers

7. **Interoperability:** no proprietary application layers

## 1.5.4. IEEE 802.15.4 based communication networks

The IEEE 802.15.4 standard defines a reliable low power low data rate communication link that is used as the underlying layers for a variety of different home automation communication network technologies. The specification leaves plenty of room for proprietary implementation because it only specifies the radio layer. This limits the benefit of the specification of the common use of the same hardware that can result in lower prices. Indeed IEEE 802.15.4 radios are the by far most deployed small band radios thanks to this benefit. A lot of proprietary wireless communication solutions are based on this protocol. Since there is no definition of higher communication layers, the standard cannot be referred as complete communication network solution.

## 1.5.5. ZigBee

ZigBee is one of many communication standards that use or reference IEEE 802.15.4 as their radio layer. Essentially

## 1.5. Alternatives for wireless home control networks

ZigBee is a specification of a network layer using the IEEE 802.15.4 radio layer. When ZigBee was originally specified the application protocol specification was not covered. This results in the situation that a broad variety of ZigBee implementations coexist in the market. None of these different implementations is interoperable with other implementations of ZigBee due to the lack of a specified application layer protocol. More recently ZigBee standard has added the specification of so called profiles to cover the application layer. Unfortunately, there are many different profiles such as the Smart Energy Profile (SEP versions 1 and 2), the Home Automation Profile and the Lighting Profile hat have limited interoperability between them and to date a limited number of vendors who have adopted them.

Manufacturers are not required to follow a certain profile but have the freedom to use their own proprietary profile - e.g. application layer protocol and still refer to themselves as ZigBee.

ZigBee is a great technology for wireless communication where interoperability is not required or needed. Its therefore well adopted in proprietary solutions as often found in commercial or industrial applications. In residential homes, where typically different devices and solutions from different manufacturers must interoperate in one network, ZigBee due to its many non-interoperable profiles and low vendor adoption of these profiles is not a good choice and has been slow to gain acceptance where application layer interoperability is important.

1. **Reliability of communication:** usually yes

2. **Security of communication:** yes

3. **Low radio emission:** yes

4. **Simple usage:** not yet

5. **Low price:** not yet

6. **Protection of investment:** not yet

7. **Interoperability:** yes at radio layer, not yet at application layer due to too many profiles and low vendor adoption of profiles

## 1.5.6. EnOcean

EnOcean GmbH is a spin-off company from the German company, Siemens AG, founded in 2001. EnOcean actors and sensors work without battery using energy harvesting techniques, means energy generated out of thin air. The claim of battery free devices using energy from the air has great appeal in an environment oriented society. This claim however comes as its cost: The communication is not as reliable as other technologies such as ZigBee or Z-Wave and the devices are comparably costly. The low power available from energy harvesting such as piezo effect for buttons solar panels or peltier elements generating energy out of temperature differences also heavily limits the wireless range of EnOcean. The company offers however repeaters to overcome this restriction. The low radio range and low communication security caused by the lack of energy make EnOcean only interesting in application where security and range is less important. This is the case for light control, particularly in industrial buildings, where the company has its sweet spot. EnOcean tries to enter the residential market but the higher price of the components has blocked the road so far.

1. **Reliability of communication:** no

2. **Security of communication:** no

3. **Low radio emission:** yes

4. **Simple usage:** yes

5. **Low price:** no

6. **Protection of investment:** yes

7. **Interoperability:** yes

## 1.5.7. Z-Wave

Z-Wave was particularly designed as wireless communication technology for residential homes. No wonder that it has all the ingredients to perfectly service this market place. The main advantages of Z-Wave are

- Used sub 1GHz frequency avoiding the heavily congested 2.4 GHz and 5 GHz bands where WLAN and ZigBee are positioned.

- Offers secure and reliable two way communication using message acknowledgement and mesh networking (for definition and explanation of mesh network please refer to 2.7)

- Comes at a reasonable price point, certainly higher than the low end analog technologies but substantially lower than high end technologies such as EnOcean that are dedicated to professional building market.

- Z-Wave ensures 100 % interoperability as its core value. All devices that implement Z-Wave will work together in one single network and can be controlled from every controller that use Z-Wave as well.

1. **Reliability of communication:** yes

2. **Security of communication:** yes

3. **Low radio emission:** yes

4. **Simple usage:** yes

5. **Low price:** not yet

6. **Protection of investment:** yes

7. **Interoperability:** yes

Figure 1.6 shows a comparison of the different wireless radio technologies in terms of their energy consumption and price point.

Table 1.1 summarizes the pros and cons of the different protocols.

## 1.6. History of Z-Wave

Z-Wave is a development of the Danish company called Zen-Sys. Two Danish engineers founded Zen-Sys at the

| Technology | Pro | Con |
|---|---|---|
| Analog | inexpensive | Unreliable, not interoperable |
| Digital | Proprietary | Not interoperable |
| WLAN | Widely used, available in cell phones, etc, low price | Not interoperable, high energy consumption / no batteries possible |
| ZigBee | Stable standard, lots low cost chips | Not interoperable |
| Z-Wave | Interoperable, reliable | Cost higher than analog systems, not (yet) available in notebooks, cell phones, ... |
| Encoean | No batteries, interoperable | High price, low security |

Table 1.1.: Summary of Pros and Cons of different radio
technologies

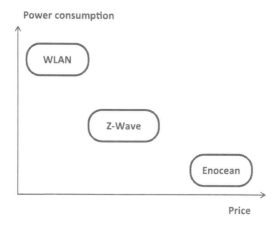

Figure 1.6.: Comparison    between    different    radio
technologies

end of the 1990's. From the initial idea of developing heir
own home automation solution the company soon evolved
into becoming a communications technology provider selling
to companies that wanted to develop interoperable control
solutions. Making this reliable. interoperable technology
available to manufacturers world-wide has resulted in the
largest ecosystem of manufacturers with compatible products.

In Figure 1.7 a Zen-Sys radio chip is illustrated. The first
generation of Zen-Sys hardware was sold from 2003 - at that
time still as a combination of a standard microcontroller
(Atmel) and a radio transceiver. This hardware platform
was extended during the following years with the chip generations 100 (2003), 200 (2005), 300 (2007), 400 (2009) and

Figure 1.7.: Zen-Sys radio chip Series 400

last 500 (2012).

Zen-Sys found the first big customers in the USA where - thanks to an early powerline carrier home automation protocol called X10 - a relevant market and market awareness already existed for home automation.

The first larger Z-Wave device manufacturer in Europe was the German switch manufacturer Merten (now a part of Schneider Electric), which publicly introduced the Z-Wave based lighting system CONNECT in the end of 2007 [Merten2007]. Since beginning of 2009 the market dynamics has strongly increased in US and Europe and Z-Wave is finding more and more adopters in Asia. This is also fostered by the purchase of Zen-Sys by the much larger US based chip manufacturer Sigma Designs.

Figure 1.8 shows the Z-Wave Alliance Website. One other landmark of the Z-Wave development was the foundation of

## 1. Introduction

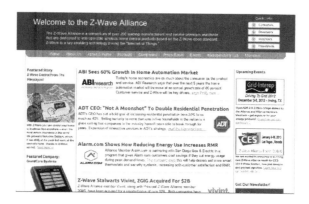

Figure 1.8.: Z-Wave Alliance Website (as of 2013)

the Z-Wave Alliance in 2005. In this industrial Alliance the manufacturers of Z-Wave compatible products are gathered. The Alliance had more than 200 manufacturers in the end of 2009. The Z-Wave Alliance enhances the standard and also takes care of central marketing events such as trade shows. Another central duty of the Z-Wave Alliance is the maintenance of the interoperability of the devices on the basis of the Z-Wave protocol. This is guaranteed by a certification program, which results in a logo on the device guaranteeing the compliance to the Z-Wave standard.

This logo is shown by Figure 1.9.

While all manufacturers base their products on the hardware of Sigma Designs, they have some freedom to implement application.

Sigma Designs defines the radio level with the line encodings and also defines the functions to organize the network itself. Precompiled firmware libraries accomplish this. The

Figure 1.9.: Z-Wave Compatibility Program

manufacturers cannot change them. Z-Wave also defines application specific functions (e.g. switch A is switched when button B is pressed) but the manufacturers are responsible to implement this. Most manufacturers optimize and enhance functions on application layer.

Hence, the certification process focuses to make sure that the application layer functions of the device comply with the standard to allow and guarantee interoperability across functionality and manufacturers boundaries.

## 1.7. Z-Wave becomes open standard

Initially, Z-Wave started as a proprietary system only available to those manufacturers that agreed with the original supplier Zen-Sys to design products based on Zen-Sys Technology.

With the adoption of the Z-Wave technology in the market and the increasing success of Z-Wave as an eco system the technology has opened up more and more.

The first step into this direction was certainly the incorporation of the Z-Wave Alliance that now acts as the central marketing engine and collection of vendors in the market. About 200 different companies from all parts of the world have joined the Alliance since its start in 2005. An interesting fact is the broad diversity of the Alliance. World market leaders are found beside little start ups and companies from different backgrounds such as security, marketing, light switches, plastic molding, TV, remote control business, software, test house etc. are all lined up in support of this interoperable standard.

The next step in opening up the Z-Wave world was the availability of a second source for the Z-Wave SOC chip. In 2011 Mitsumi from Japan announced the availability of a certified SOC from its factories. [Mitsumi2011]

In 2012 Z-Wave became an open and public standard. The radio and MAC laser were standardized as standard G.9959 by the international telecommunication union ITU-T. [ITU2012]

# 2. Radio Layer

## 2.1. Wireless Basics

In an ideal situation, radio waves spread out steadily like light waves in all directions, generating a spherical field. For technical applications the wavelength ($\lambda$) and the frequency ($f$) are related to each other with the formula:

$$\lambda = \frac{c}{f}$$

In contrast to infrared light, or light waves in general, radio waves can penetrate in ceilings, walls, pieces, of furniture and other objects. Such obstacles however weaken the radio signal and reduce the range.

If wireless components are installed its recommended to keep as few obstacles between the sender and the receiver. In practice, this means that wireless components should not be installed in random places. The ability of radio signals to penetrate walls and other obstacles depends on the frequency of the signal. In general, radio frequencies below 1 Ghz have a higher ability to penetrate walls than e.g. signals in the 2.4 GHz, a frequency used by commonly known technologies such as WLAN or Zigbee.

Image 2.1 illustrates the attenuation of radio signals by a wall.

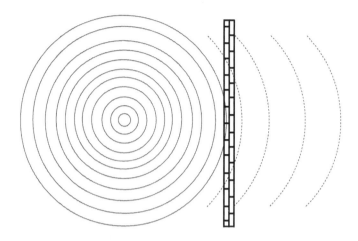

Figure 2.1.: Attenuation of radio signals by a wall

## 2.2. Frequencies used by Z-Wave

Z-Wave typically uses license free but regulated frequency bands. The first is important from the cost point of view, the second ensures a fair usage of the frequency band and therefore reliable transmission even for low energy wireless technologies such as Z-Wave. Radio frequency regulation is unfortunately a governmental task and hence different countries have applied different regulations to radio frequencies in their respective jurisdiction.

Table 2.1 shows the different frequencies in different countries and the underlying national or international specifications.

There is one multinational regulation driven by the CEPT

| Region | Standard | Z-Wave Frequency |
|---|---|---|
| Australia | AS/NZS 4268 | 921.4 MHz |
| Brazil | ANATEL Resolution 506 | 921.4 MHz |
| CEPT* | EN 300 220 | 868.4 MHz |
| China | TBD | 868.4 MHz |
| Hong Kong | HKTA 1035 | 919.8 MHz |
| India | N/A | 865.2 MHz |
| Japan 950 | ARIB T96 | 951-956 MHz |
| Japan 920 | ARIB STD-T108 | 922-926 MHz |
| Malaysia | N/A | 868.1 MHz |
| Mexico | FCC CFR47 Part 15.249 | 908.4 MHz |
| New Zealand | AS/NZS 4268 | 921.4 MHz |
| Russia | GKRCh/EN 300 220 | 869.0 MHz |
| Singapore | TS SRD/EN 300 220 | 868.4 MHz |
| South Africa | ICASA/EN 300 220 | 868.4 MHz |
| UAE | EN 300 220 | 868.4 MHz |
| USA/Canada | FCC CFR47 Part 15.249 | 908.4 MHz |

Table 2.1.: Different Frequencies allocated to Z-Wave in different countries and the underlying National or International approval document

organization.

" The European Conference of Postal and
Telecommunications Administrations (CEPT)
was established on June 26, 1959, as a co-
ordinating body for European state telecommunications and postal organizations. The
acronym comes from the French version
of its name Confrence europenne des administrations des postes et des tlcommu-
nications. CEPT was responsible for the
creation of the European Telecommunications Standards Institute (ETSI) in 1988.
[CEPT]"

48 countries are members of CEPT (2012): Albania, An-
dorra, Austria, Azerbaijan, Belarus, Belgium, Bosnia and
Herzegovina, Bulgaria, Croatia, Cyprus,Czech Republic, Den-
mark, Estonia, Finland, France, Georgia, Germany, Greece,
Hungary, Iceland, Ireland, Italy, Latvia, Liechtenstein, Lithua-
nia, Luxembourg, Macedonia, Malta, Moldova, Monaco,
Montenegro,Netherlands, Norway, Poland, Portugal, Roma-
nia, Russian Federation, San Marino, Serbia, Slovakia,Slovenia,
Spain, Sweden, Switzerland, Turkey, Ukraine, United King-
dom and Vatican City. All of them with the exception of
Russian Federation have agreed to set a license-free band
called **SRD 860 (Short Range Devices)** in the frequency range of 863 ... 870 MHz. This band has been
allocated for license-free operation using FHSS[1], DSSS [2], or

---

[1]Frequency Hopping Spread Spectrum
[2]Direct Sequence Spread Spectrum

| Frequency | Duty cycle | ERP |
|---|---|---|
| 863-865 MHz | 100% (wireless audio) | 10 mW |
| 863.0 - 865.6 MHz | 0.1% or LBT+AFA | 25 mW |
| 865.0 - 868.0 MHz | 1% or LBT+AFA | 25 mW |
| 868.0 - 868.6 MHz | 1% or LBT+AFA | 25 mW |
| 868.7 - 869.2 MHz | 0.1% or LBT+AFA | 25 mW |
| 869.4 - 869.65 MHz | 10% or LBT+AFA, 25 kHz channel spacing | 500 mW |
| 869.7 - 870.0 MHz | 100% (voice communication) | 5 mW |

Table 2.2.: Structure of the frequency band

analog modulation with either a transmission duty cycle of 0.1%, 1% or 10% depending on the band, or **Listen Before Talk (LBT)** with **Adaptive Frequency Agility (AFA)**.

The structure of this frequency band is shown in table 2.2.

Z-Wave is using the frequency of 868.4 MHz resp. 868.42 MHz in all CEPT countries except Russian Federation. The Z-Wave radio transmission is therefore limited to 25 mW maximum transmitting power and a duty cycle of 1 %. The broad acceptance of this frequency band due to the CEPT regulation has caused more states in Asia and Africa to accept this frequency for Z-Wave although they are not member of the CEPT organization. Figure 2.2 shows all the

Figure 2.2.: Members of the CEPT-Accord in Europe

members of the CEPT-Accord in Europe.

In North America the so called ISM (Industry Science Medicine Band) with a frequency of 908 MHz is used for and licensed for Z-Wave. The 908 MHz is also limited both in terms of maximum transmitting power and duty cycle.

## 2.3. Wireless Distance Estimations

In general wireless home networks can be installed without extensive planning. Proper planning however will reduce the chance for disappointments and problems later on during operations. The following sections shall give some recommendations and outline some typical challenges of wireless communication.

These aspects of communication shall be taken into consideration:

- Direct distances between different communication nodes

- Effective wall thicknesses

- Shielding material

- Attenuation or other negative impact by building material and furnishing

## 2.3.1. Antenna

The maximum distance to bridge with a wireless technology is specified by product and depends on

- the radio frequency

- the transmitting power and - not to forget

- the antenna and

- the antenna coupling to the transceiver.

Assuming a good antenna with perfect coupling of the antenna, a distance of up to 200 m with free sight can be bridged using the Z-Wave technology.

In terms of antenna there are three typical solutions.

1: A professional dedicated antenna for the Z-Wave frequency certainly results in the best transmission results. However, these antennas are expensive and bulky. Figure 2.3 demonstrates such a dedicated Z-Wave antenna on an industrial Z-Wave Gateway.

2. Very often a simple wire of a defined length of $\lambda/4$ is used in Z-Wave devices as shown in Figure 2.4. The wires

Figure 2.3.: Dedicated Z-Wave Antenna on an industrial Z-Wave Gateway

Figure 2.4.: Dedicated wire as Z-Wave antenna

have a much worse radio performance but still do well in typical smart home environments.

3. PCBA Antenna. The simplest way to implement an antenna is to use a piece of copper or trace on the printed circuit board, hence the name PCBA antenna. This sort of antenna can be seen in Figure 2.5. If done well these antenna can have the same performance as an external wire but will never reach the performance of a dedicated external antenna. Wireless distances based on PCBA antenna or simple wires are about 100 m but still depend on the antenna coupling to the rest of the circuitry, where poor designs can cause further degradation of the radio signal.

Figure 2.5.: PCBA antenna

## 2.3.2. Attenuation

The radio signal is further attenuated by obstacles between the sender and the receiver. Whenever there is an obstacle in direct line of sight between the transmitter and receiver, the resulting distance will be shorter than the maximum distance achievable with the given antenna. The attenuation depends on the material of the obstacle and the corresponding ability of the radio frequency to penetrate this material.

Table 2.3 shows the percentage attenuation of a radio signal depending on the material using a typical thickness of this material.

These factors allow calculating the typical maximum radio distance between transmitter and receiver using the data given in table 2.4

| Nr. | Material | Thickness | Attenuation |
|---|---|---|---|
| 2 | Plaster | < 10 cm | 10 % |
| 3 | Glass (without metal coating) | < 5 cm | 10 % |
| 4 | Stone | < 30 cm | 30 % |
| 5 | Pumice | < 30 cm | 10 % |
| 6 | Aerated concrete stone | < 30 cm | 20 % |
| 7 | Red brick | < 30 cm | 35 % |
| 8 | Iron-reinforced concrete | < 30 cm | 30 ...90 % |
| 9 | Ceiling | < 30 cm | 70 % |
| 10 | Outer wall | < 30 cm | 60 % |
| 11 | Inner wall | < 30 cm | 40 % |
| 12 | Metal grid | < 1 mm | 90 % |
| 13 | Aluminium coating | < 1 mm | 100 % |

Table 2.3.: Attenuation of different material[Merten2008]

| Obstacle | Act. Distance | Type | Attenuation | New distance |
|---|---|---|---|---|
| No 1 | 30 m | Concrete | 30% | 21 m |
| Take new value to next step | | | | |
| No 2 | 21 m | Glass | 10% | 18,90 m |
| Take new value to next step | | | | |
| No 3 | 18,9 m | Plaster wall | 10% | 17 m |
| Take new value to next step | | | | |
| | 17 m | | | |

Table 2.4.: Work Sheet to determine the wireless distance

If the radio signal penetrates the obstacle at an obleak angle (other than 90 degrees), then the attenuation effect will be increased. If the range calculated in the end is longer than the measured distance between transmitter and receiver, the components should function well. Pieces of furniture, device mounting, metal coatings, plantings and high air humidity should all be considered when planning the best route for your wireless system. Because these attenuations are approximate, a test is recommended before the fixed installation is made.

## 2.3.3. Distances to other wireless signal sources

Radio receivers should be attached in a distance of minimum 30 cm from other radio sources. Examples of radio sources are:

- Computers

- Microwave devices

- Electronic transformers

- Audio equipment and video equipment

- Pre-coupling devices for fluorescent lamps

The distance to other wireless transmitters like cordless phones or audio radio transmissions should be at least 3 metres. As well as this, the following radio sources should be taken into account:

- Disturbances by switch of electric motors and other inductive loads

- Interference by defective electrical appliances

- Disturbances by HF welding apparatuses

- Medical treatment devices.

## 2.3.4. Effective thickness of walls

The locations of transmitter and receiver should be selected in such a way that the direct connecting line only runs on a very short distance through material, which causes attenuation.

Figure 2.6 demonstrates the effective wall thickness.

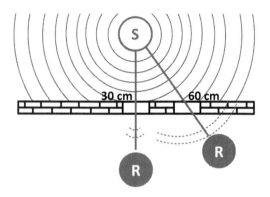

Figure 2.6.: Effective wall thickness

## 2.3.5. Wireless Shadows

Metallic parts of the building or pieces of furniture shield the electromagnetic waves. Behind a structure like this, there may be a so-called radio shadow as shown in Figure 2.7, where no direct reception is possible.

Despite radio shadow, it is possible for wireless signals to be reflected by metal structures and still reach the final destination. Reflections are unpredictable and it is recommended that you test your systems before permanent installation.

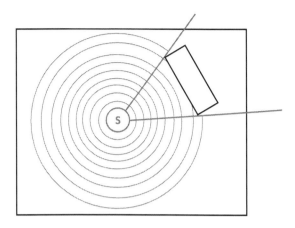

Figure 2.7.: Radio shadow by metallic structures

## 2.3.6. Reflections

Reflections are used by amateur radio connections to bridge big distances (several thousand kilometers with relatively low power) in the short wave band. On this occasion, the reflective property of the ionosphere is used. Within buildings reflections may cause disturbances or attenuation if the original and the reflected way are received together. The receipt of the original transmissio and one or more of its reflections is commonly refered to as multi-path as the signals travel by multiple paths on their way to the receiver.

## 2.3.7. Interference

Figure 2.8 illustrates the signal gain by interference. Interference can occur in different phase situations that are

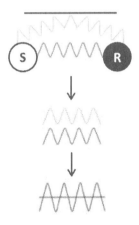

Figure 2.8.: Signal gain by constructive or in-phase interference

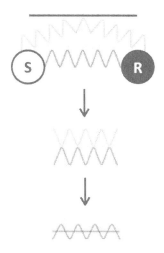

Figure 2.9.: Signal attenuation by destructive or out-of-phase interference

caused by different run times and by the way the radio waves are increased or attenuated.

Figure 2.9 shows the signal attenuation by destructive interference. Interference can be resolved by changing the positions of the transmitter or receiver slightly. Even a couple of centimeters may work. It really is a process of trial and error to see what works for you in your home.

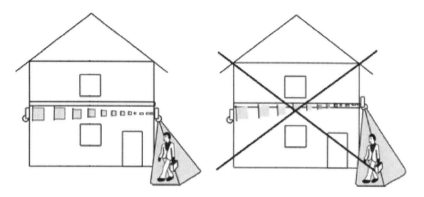

Figure 2.10.: Challenge of mounting height

### 2.3.8. Relevance of Mounting Heights

If motion detectors are mounted outside the house, the assembly height is critical. If the motion detector is mounted at the same height as the interior floor or ceiling level, then the radio signal has to penetrate the building material of the floor or ceiling. This will be ineffective as this will result in very high attenuation of the signal.

This challenge of mounting height is demonstrated in Figure 2.10.

## 2.4. Electro Magnetic Energy (EME) and Health

From infrared, to Bluetooth, to Z-Wave, there are numerous wireless messages flying through the air. There is a general concern whether or not this can affect users health. Radi-

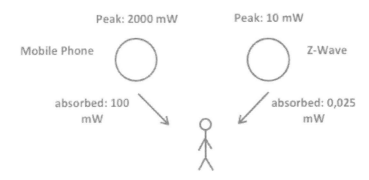

Figure 2.11.: Transmitting power of Z-Wave compared to cell phone

ation power from radio transmitters is a critical factor. As most of us use mobile phones, a comparison can be drawn. Mobile phones transmit a constant radio signal with a peak energy of 2000 mW into the brain when held next to the ear. Without any other protection and mostly operating next to the ear, a person will absorbe about 100 mW of energy into his head. This exposure continues throughout the whole telephone call! Z-Wave presents nowhere near such a threat as mobile phones. The system works with peak transmission powers of 10mW and this power level is only applied for 1 % of the time (duty cycle = 1 %). This corresponds to an average radiation power of only 0.1 mW. In addition to this much lower radiated power, it is rare that a Z-Wave transmitter in let's say a remote control or motion detector operates directly in or close to the body.

Figure 2.11 shows the direct comparison between the transmitting power of Z-Wave and a cell phone.

The signal attenuation that is generated in a distance of only 1m causes another reduction of the radiation power around the factor of 40. The human body is only hit by a radiation power of 0.025 mW. This is about 1: 4000 lower than the emission of a mobile phone. Taking further into account that the radio signal will only be transmitted during a short period of time when a button is pressed or a sensor signal is transmitted, the electromagnetically emission of a Z-Wave network does not contribute to the general electromagnetic pollution in a home and does not have any negative effect to human beings.

# 2.5. Z-Wave Networking

# 2.6. Data Communication via G.9959

Z-Wave is using its designated frequencies in a standardized way. This standard is issued by the ITU T under the number G.9959 [ITU2012]. This standard uses two terms to describe the communication:

- The physical layer defines the way the frequency is used and how certain bits are encoded and transmitted.

- The media access control defines how a whole frame can be transported from one device to another device via the wireless link.

## 2.6.1. The PHY function

The PHY function defines how to transport a set of bytes from a transmitter to a receiver.

Z-Wave is not bound to a certain frequency but is using the recommended frequencies defined in chapter 2.2. Depending on the frequencies different line encodings and line speeds are used.

Z-Wave uses frequency shift keying, also referred to as FSK. To encode bits, this means that a logical 0 is transmitted by sending a signal on one frequency and a logical 1 is transmitted by using a different frequency. This means the Z-Wave transmitter is either sending on frequency A or on frequency B or not sending at all. The difference between the two frequencies is 40 KHz. In case of the European or

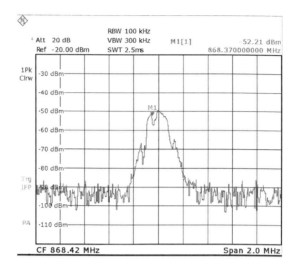

Figure 2.12.: Frequency Spectrum

CEPT frequency with a center of 868.42 MHz this means that the real frequencies used for transmission are either 868.40 MHz or 868.44 Mhz.

The frequency difference for a FSK is a tradeoff between two goals. The two frequencies shall be far enough away from each other to make sure that a receiver can easily distinguish a '0' from a '1' in a noisy environment. On the other hand they need to be close enough to make sure that one single antenna filter (designed for the frequency in the middle between the two frequencies) is not attenuating the two signal for '0' and '1' too much. Also local regulations limit the spread or spacing of these two frequencies so that availabe frequency allocation is optimized.

Figure 2.12 shows a measured frequency spectrum of a

Z-Wave transmitter under real conditions with background noise. It is easy to see that with a simple filter it is possible to filter real 0 and 1 out of such a spectrum. The receiving part of the Z-Wave link needs to apply certain filters to find the right frequencies and to decode the data that was sent.

Historically, Z-Wave used a data rate of 9.6 kb/s. Since this is more than sufficient for small commands like turning on or off a switch, more complicated functions like firmware updating or transmission of metering values need a higher speed.

In later versions of the Z-Wave protocol a 40 kbit/s data rate was added to the protocol. Certain implementations even support 100 kb/s. However 40 kb/s is the standard data rate today while 100 kbit/s will be used in future implementtions. To make it easier for the receiver to distinguish between different bit rates Z-Wave defines different line encoding. The 9.6 Kb/s data rate uses a Manchester encoding while 40 Kb/s and 100 kb/s data are encoded with NRZ (Non Return Zero).

Figure 2.13 shows the difference between the two encodings.

In Manchester encoding a logical 0 is the change from the lower frequency to the higher frequency while in NRZ encoding the frequency itself defines the bit value.

Both encodings are very robust and therefore well suited for a home environment with much noise and high requirement for reliability.

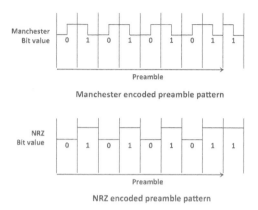

Figure 2.13.: NRZ versus Manchester encoding

## 2.6.2. Framing

In order to allow the receiver to find the right 0s and 1s the transmitter needs to send a well known pattern prior to the actual data. This so called preamble is used to synchronize the receiver with the transmitter. The preamble is a sequence of 0-1-0-1-0-1-0-1 that is repeated a minimum of 10 times. After the preamble there is a so called start of frame delimiter. This byte is signaling that the data part of the frame is starting. After these actual data is sent, the whole communication is concluded with an end of frame delimiter of one byte.

Figure 2.14 shows the basic frame as defined in ITU-T G.9959 res. Z-Wave. The maximum user date size is defined as 64 bytes. Later on in chapter 3 and 4 it is explained that the minimum user data size is 13 bytes. This allows some calculation:

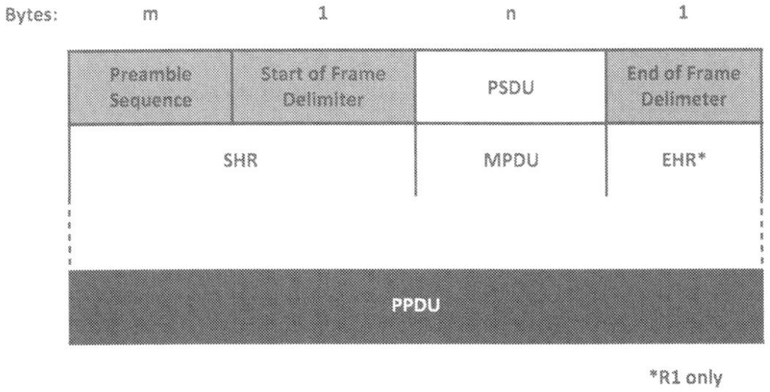

Figure 2.14.: Frame Format for PHY Layer

| Frame size | at 9.6 kbit/s | at 40 kbit/s |
|------------|---------------|--------------|
| 25 bytes   | 20 ms         | 5 ms         |
| 76 bytes   | 63 ms         | 15 ms        |

Table 2.5.: Transmission times of minimal and maximal PHY frames

The total frame size including preamble, data, start of frame delimiter and end of frame delimiter is 10 bytes + 1 byte + 13 bytes ... 64 bytes + 1 byte = 25 bytes ... 76 bytes.

Table 2.5 shows the different times needed to transmit Z-Wave frames with the different frequencies

61

## 2.6.3. Home ID and Node ID

A wireless communication network needs to make sure that a certain data element is transported from the right sender to the right receiver. This means that a receiver needs to be able to find out

- what data elements are to be received and

- what data elements are not addressed to it and should be ignored.

The second point is particularly important if multiple wireless networks are operated within the same physical location. As soon as different networks overlap, e.g. houses or apartments that are close to each other, the wireless network protocol needs to make sure that data stays within the originating network and is only received by a receiver that is also a member of the originating network. All data of foreign networks must be rejected. Within a single network the wireless protocol needs to make sure that the specific receiver of a data message knows that this message is for them and not for a different device in the same network.

In order to accomplish both tasks the general rule in a network is:

> **All devices in a network need to have *something* in common and they need to have *something* that is individual for each and every device.**

In wired networks the *something in common* is typically the access to the same wire. All devices connected to this wire belong to the same network. In the wireless world there is no wire. There are two different ways to solve the problem:

- Every device has a unique identifier. This identifier is assigned at the time of manufacture.

- Only 'master' or 'inclusion' devices have a unique identifier assigned and the time of manufacture and all other devices ship 'dumb' or devoid of identifier.

In a technology that uses unique addresses each device that gets ever manufactured needs to have one single unique numerical ID to distinguish it from all other devices in existence. An example of this is WLANs. The unique address is here referred to a MAC address and can be found on every WLAN router or other WLAN devices. The advantage of this approach is that the network management can never fail and devices can always be distinguished from other devices in the same or another network. The price for this approach is that every device in a network needs to maintain a list of the addresses of all other devices in the same network. This consumes memory and may take computing power if the list gets long and needs to be searched.

Z-Wave has therefore chosen a different way. Only master or 'inclusion' devices have unique identifiers. all other devices are empty or 'dumb' . When a master or 'inclusion' controller creates a network it shares its unique identifier with the dumb device and this becomes the Network ID or the element that all devices in this network will have in common. The master or 'inclusion' controller also assigns a sequential device or node ID so that each individual device within the same network can be identified addresses during the inclusion of a device into the network. This has advantages and disadvantages:

- A clear advantage is less need of memory and a much simpler addressing and address filtering.

- The disadvantage is that in case the controller does something wrong, there may be two devices with similar addresses in one network creating confusion.

The Z-Wave protocol defines two identifications for the organization of the network:

- The Home ID is the common identification of all nodes belonging to one logical Z-Wave network. It has a length of 4 bytes = 32 bits.

- The Node ID is the address of the single node [3] within the network. The Node ID has a length of 1 byte = 8 bits. Since a few node Ids are reserved for internal network organization functions, Z-Wave allows to address 232 different nodes within one wireless network.

Nodes of different Home IDs do not belong to the same network and cannot communicate with each other. Its therefore not a problem to have more than one device with the same Node ID in one room as long as they have different Home IDs, hence belong to different networks.

Certain Z-Wave devices are called controllers because they are able to assign their own Home ID to other nodes and

---

[3]Devices in a network are also referred to as nodes. Since the term Node ID used this wording all devices will be referred here as nodes as well.

also assign a network-wide individual Node ID to the same node. All other devices are called slaves because they don't have a valid Home ID they can assign to other devices.

Z-Wave controllers can exist in different shapes:

- as a remote control,

- as PC software in conjunction with a Z-Wave transceiver connected in the PC (typically via USB),

- as a gateway or as

- a wall switch with special controller function.

> Important: A Z-Wave controller is a controller because it can assign his own Home ID to other devices and also assigns an individual Node ID. Slaves are Z-Wave devices that can not assign their own Home ID and can not assign Node IDs.

The Home ID of a controller cannot be changed by the user and becomes the common Home ID of all devices, which were included by this controller.

The controller that begins to build up a network is transferring its Home ID to other devices and becomes the designated primary controller of this network. In a bigger network several controllers can work together, but there is always only one controller with the privilege to assign Ids - the primary controller. All other controllers are called secondary controllers.

The primary controller includes other nodes into the network by assigning them its own Home ID. If a node accepts

| | Definition | In the Controller | In the Slave |
|---|---|---|---|
| Home ID | The Home ID is the common identification of a Z-Wave network | The Home ID is already available at factory default. | No Home ID at factory default |
| Node ID | The Node ID is the individual identification (address) of a node within a common network | Controller has its own Node ID predefined (typically 0x01) | Is assigned by the primary controller |

Table 2.6.: Home ID versus Node ID

the Home Id of the primary controller this node becomes part of the network. Together with assigning the Home Id the primary controller also assigns an individual Node Id to the new included device. This process is referred to as Inclusion.

*Note: The definition and the process to use Home Id and Node Id is part of the ITU-T G.9959. However the process how to assign Home Id and Node Id - the inclusion process - remains intellectual property of Sigma Designs (for more information about the legal situation of Z-Wave please refer to Chapter 5.1).*

In Figure 2.15 four devices are available in factory default state. There are two controllers with a preset Home Id. Two other devices cannot operate as a controller (slave) and, hence, have no own Home Id.

Depending on which of the controllers is used to build up a Z-Wave network, the network Home ID in this example will be either 0x00001111 or 0x00002222.

Both controllers have the same Node ID 1. The slave devices do not have any Node ID assigned. In theory this picture shows two networks with one node in each of them. Because none of the nodes in the figure has any common Home ID, no communication can take place.

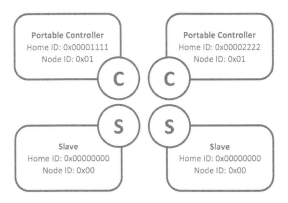

Figure 2.15.: Z-Wave devices before inclusion in a network

One of the two controllers is now selected as being the primary controller of the network. This controller assigns his Home ID to all the other devices (includes them) and also assigns them individual Node ID . The second controller assumes the same Home ID as the inclusion or primary controller.

After successful inclusion all nodes have the same Home ID, i.e. they are connected in one network with each other. At the same time every node has a different individual Node ID. Only with this individual Node IDs they can be distinguished from each other and can communicate with each other. In a Z-Wave network nodes having a common Home ID must not have the same Node ID.

In the network shown as an example in Figure 2.16 there are two controllers. The controller whose Home ID became

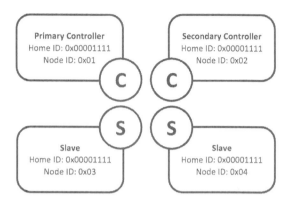

Figure 2.16.: Network after successful Inclusion

the Home ID of all devices is the primary controller. All other controllers become so called secondary controllers.

A secondary controller is also a controller from the technical point of view and does not differ from the primary controller. However, only the controller with the privilege being the primary controller can include further devices. (If a SIS is present every controller can include device by executing the node id assignment done by the SIS. For more information about SIS please refer to Chapter 2.10.2)

Because the nodes of different networks can't communicate with each other due to the different Home Id, they can coexist and do not even see each other. This is shown in Figure 2.17.

The 32 bit long Home ID allows to distinguish up to 4 billion ($2^{32}$) different Z-Wave to networks with a maximum

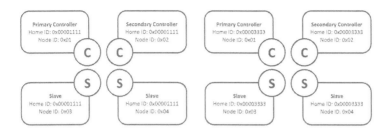

Figure 2.17.: Two Z-Wave-Network with different Home IDs coexist

number of $2^8 = 256$ different nodes.

It is not possible for one single node has two different Home IDs or Node IDs. There are devices (so called bridge controllers) that allow bridging two different networks but they consist of two independent Z-Wave nodes with an interconnection at a higher layer. With their individual Z-Wave networks they still appear as a simple node.

## 2.6.4. Media Access Function - MAC

After looking at the way the networks are identified and the way nodes are identified within the network next we need to explore the way data is sent over the air. This is managed by the next layer in the Layered ISO communications stack, the Media Access Controller. in short MAC.

The MAC function uses up to 64 bytes of the PHY frame to transport network relevant data plus the application data itself. The allocation of the bytes of the PHY frame is again defined as a frame, now the MAC frame.

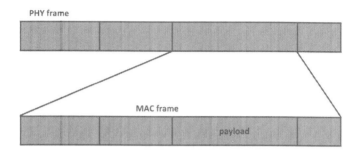

Figure 2.18.: MAC Frame within PHY Frame

Figure 2.18 shows how the MAC frame fits into the PHY frame and Figure 2.19 shows the definition of the MAC frame according to the specification ITU-T G.9959 resp. Z-Wave.

The MAC frame consists of the following data elements:

- Home ID  4 bytes

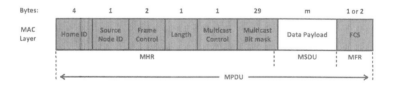

Figure 2.19.: MAC Frame Layout

| Byte | Bit | Function |
|------|-----|----------|
| 1 | 0...3 | Header type |
| 1 | 4 | Speed |
| 1 | 5 | Low power flag |
| 1 | 6 | Ack / Req |
| 1 | 7 | Routed |
| 2 | 0...3 | Sequence number |
| 2 | 5... | Beam Control |

Table 2.7.: Bit Assignment of MAC Frame

- Source Node ID  1 byte

- Frame Control  2 bytes

- Frame Length 1 byte

- Destination Node ID  1 byte

- Data Payload  up to 54 bytes

- Frame Checksum - 1 byte

All Z-wave data packets in the network are identified by their Home IDs and the Node IDs of sender and receiver. The other data elements are used to either manage the packet itself (length, checksum) or to control the flow of packets in the network. This task is accomplished by the frame control bytes. They have the following structure:

**Frame control**  Table 2.7 shows the bits of the frame header

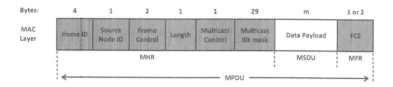

Figure 2.20.: Multicast Frame Layout

The MAC frame needs 10 bytes out of the 64 bytes of the PHY frame for its own purposes, leaving just 54 bytes for the real payload data of the application.

**Singlecast** Beside the so called point-to-point connection or single cast where each packet has a source or sender Node ID and a destination or receiver Node ID, there are other ways to communicate:

**Broadcast** All packets sent to the Node ID (255 = 0xff) are considered as broadcast. This means they are received by all nodes in the network. The frame format of a broadcast frame does not differ from the frame format of a single cast or point-to-point frame.

**Multicast** In a multicast communication one sender sends a data packet to multiple recipients. While this is always achievable by sending multiple identical single cast packets to a list of destinations, the multicast operation simplifies and accelerates such a function. In a multicast frame the field of the destination Node Id is replaced by a node mask

72

where each Node Id in the network is represented by a single bit (see Figure2.20). Obviously this Node Id mask allocates more than a single byte for the destination address but 29 bytes. This leaves only 26 bytes as payload for the application. Nevertheless the use of multicasts may be recommended for certain communication patterns.

## 2.6.5. Data Reliability and Error Correction

In order to verify that the data packet was received correctly, an 8 bit checksum byte is added to the data frame. This checksum covers the whole frame and a frame is only considered a valid frame if this checksum is detected as correct.

The checksum is calculated in a very simple way. It is just combining all bytes of the frame (from Home Id to the last byte prior to the checksum itself) using an exclusive OR. In the programming language C this algorithm can be describes as:

Listing 2.1: Z-Wave Check Sum in C

```
1 Byte GenerateCheckSum (Byte *Data, Byte Length)
2 {
3        Byte checksum = 0xff;
4        for (; Length > 0; Length --) checksum ^= *Data++;
5        return checksum;
6 }
```

This simple checksum algorithm and the fact that this single byte needs to protect up to 63 bytes of data is clearly a weakness of Z-Wave as for almost all other wireless protocols that were designed for home control. A much stronger protection of the data was therefore introduced later on as a feature of the application layer (see chapter 4.3.7) A simple example shall illustrate this fact:

Lets assume a data stream of the two bytes 0x01 and 0x80 (the first byte has only the least significant byte as 1, all others are 0, the next byte only has the most significant byte as 1, the others are zero.

The Z-Wave checksum algorithm will use the start value of 0xff, run two iterations and generate a checksum byte of 0b01111110 or 0x7f. In case the two bytes of the data stream are just twisted to 0x01, 0x80 the very same checkusm algorithm will generate the very same checksum of 0b01111110 or 0x7f.

This shows that such a weak algorithm is hardly able to detect small changes in the data packet. The checksum has only $1 : 2^8$ or $1 : 256$ different values, hence the chance that a random dat stream is wrongly detected as valid frame is also $1 : 2^8$ or $1 : 256$.

The situation in Z-Wave is less critical because a frame will only be accepted by the receiver if

- the checksum is correct **and**

- the Home Id of 4 Byte is matching the Home id of the receiving device **and**

- the Node Id of 1 Byte is matching the Node id of the receiving device.

This results in a chance of $1 : 2^{42}$ that a random byte stream will be accepted as valid frame and used for the application.

In many wireless communication networks a communication between a sender and a receiver is accomplished by simply sending a message over the air from source to destination. In case this message gets lost (due to interference or positioning the receiver too far away from the sender), the sender does not get any feedback if the message was received and the receiver was able to execute the command properly. This may result in stability problems and frustrate the user of such a network. In Z-Wave the receiver has to acknowledge every command sent by the transmitter. This gives an indication whether the communication was successful or not.

> A communication in Z-Wave was successful if the sending data packet (1) was received with correct checksum (2) and correct Home Id (3) and correct Node Id by the receiver AND the sender (4) has received an acknowledgement packet again (5) with correct checksum and (6) correct Home Id and (7) correct Node Id - from the destination.

The process can be illustrated by comparing it with the traditional main service.

Not having acknowledged messages is like sending a normal standard letter to a destination. In most of the cases this letter will be delivered correctly and the receiver will be able to read the letter. However, there is no guarantee and some uncertainty remains.

Important messages are therefore to send as **registered letter with return receipt**. Here the sender has a written

Figure 2.21.: Communication    with    and    without acknowledgement

proof that his letter was delivered correctly and handed over to the receiver.

Even a **registered letter with return receipt** does not guarantee that the letter will always be delivered correctly. However, the sender will get an indication when a receiver has for instance moved out of town and can do other actions to make sure the letter will finally reach its destination.

In Z-Wave the return receipt is called Acknowledge (ACK). If no ACK is received the transmitter will wait a random time between 20 ms and 100 ms and retry two more times. After three unsuccessful attempts the Z-Wave transceiver will give up and report a failure. The number of unsuccessful transmission attempts can be served as an indicator of the quality of wireless connection. The communication with and without acknowledgement is shown in Figure2.21.

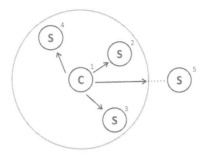

Figure 2.22.: Network without routing

The only exception from this process are broadcast messages. They must not be confirmed. Communications where an ACK is received by the sender are referred to as 'Reliable Communications'.

## 2.7. Routing

In a simple wireless communication network all devices can communicate directly over the air, they are called "in sight". This means that they are close enough together to "see" each other with their "wireless eyes". If a node - for whatever reason - drops out of sight, it is not longer reachable and all communication of this node will fail.

Figure 2.22 shows such a simple network. From the controller point of view nodes 2,3 and 4 are reachable. Node 5 however is not existent for the controller since its not in direct sight, sometimes also referred to as "in range".

In case there is no successful communication to this node 5 from the controller because this node will now be considered as non existing or gone.

If a communications network is not even using an acknowledgement, the controller will not even realize that his communication partner will never get his messages. The sender will still assume proper execution of the commands sent. This is certainly not an acceptable function of a wireless communication network and would not be considered a 'Reliable Communication'.

Z-Wave is a wireless system that offers a very powerful mechanism to overcome this limitation. Beside the confirmation of every packet sent - introduced in chapter 2.6.5 - Z-Wave nodes can also forward and repeat messages on behalf of other devices if these devices are not in direct range to each other. This gives two remarkable advantages:

- It extends the wireless range of the network because messages can reach their destination via multiple hops.

- If a communication fails, there may be a backup option - a plan B. The sender can just ask other nodes to help out and choose a different route to its desired destination.

Figure 2.23 shows the same network again with the controller as Node ID 1 communicating directly to the nodes 2,3 and 4. Node 6 lies outside of its radio range but it is within the radio range of node 2. Therefore, the controller

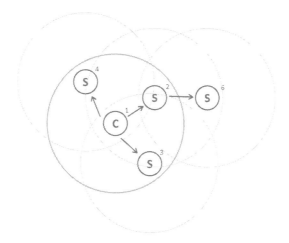

Figure 2.23.: Z-Wave network with routing

can communicate to node 6 via node 2. The way from node 1 via node 2 to node 6 is called **a route**.

A network that has various different ways to communicate between different nodes using other nodes as routers is called a **meshed network**.

Figure 2.23 illustrates another side effect of routing. In case the direct communication between node 1 and node 2 is blocked there are still other options to communicate to node 3. The controller may be able to choose node 3 as router.

It is evident that more nodes result in more routing options and therefore create a more robust or fault tolerant network.

Z-Wave is able to route message via up to four repeating nodes. This is a compromise between the network size,

Figure 2.24.: Maximum route between 2 nodes via 4 repeaters

robustness and the maximum time a message is allowed to travel in the network.

The maximum route between 2 nodes via 4 repeaters is shown in Figure 2.24.

Assuming, the maximum radio range with a good antenna is up to 200 meters. Routing could in theory extend the wireless coverage of a Z-Wave network to almost 1 kilometer. This is certainly a corner case far from reality. However, it is good to know that a Z-Wave network with its two functions 'confirmation or acknowledgement of messages' and 'routing of messages' is more than able to establish a robust network within even larger residential homes or offices.

Long routes are possible but not desirable. Let's apply some math again:

Table 2.5 has shown that a single frame of minimal size may still take about 20 ms to be transmitted. The same time is needed to transmit the returning ACK-command. Since the routers need to fully receive the whole packet before it can be resent again (store-and-forward), the travel time over a route of full length will be 5 * 2 * 20 ms = 200 ms.

In case there are more packets to be exchanged in order to execute a single function on the receiving node, the delay caused by communicating can reach a level that is perceived as too slow by the user.

Nevertheless, even if the network consists only of nodes in direct range, its good to know that the network has plenty of fall back options, just in case.

**How are routes built in a Z-Wave network ?** The primary controller of a network is responsible for building and maintaining the knowledge about routes in the network. Every node is able to determine which nodes are in direct wireless range. These nodes are called **neighbors** . During inclusion and later on request by the primary controller the nodes are able to inform the primary controller about their actual neighbor nodes. Using this information the controller is able to build a table that has all the information about possible communication routes in the network. This table is the base for determining routes between two nodes. This routes are fixed unless any change in the routing table or a failed communication forces the controller to change it Each packet, which is supposed to be sent using other nodes, has the full information about the desired route in the packet header. It is not possible to change this route on the fly during the way of the packet in the network.

While this sounds quite inflexible this is in fact quite smart. It significantly reduces traffic over the air and attempts to follow wrong routes.

If the attempt to communicate with a certain device over a given route fails (no acknowledge received back), the controller will try two more times the same route and then a number of other possible routes to reach the device. This is also very smart because the route may be interrupted by a failed or otherwise not available node but the final destination is still alive and working well.

If the communication attempt fails, the controller will try again and again to communicate with the desired target always creating a lot of traffic by testing the other available routes. This behavior is still desired but the increased traffic may slow down other communication in the network and will particularly keep the controller chip busy. A result of this traffic is the delayed executions of other wireless commands such as turning on a light.

Figures 2.25, 2.26 and 2.27 illustrate the process. In Figure 2.25 a direct communication attempt between Node S and Node R fails in three times. In Figure 2.26 the sender Node S uses a route via Node 6 but that communication fails at different points. In the first attempt the message is routed but fails to reach the final destination node. The second attempt finally reaches the node but the acknowledgement message gets lost. The third attempt via this route does not even reach the first intermediate node. The node however tries another time, now a route via Node 8.

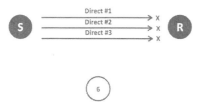

Figure 2.25.: Multiple communication attempts in Z-Wave
- step 1

This attempt succeeds in the first time, because both the message itself and the acknowledgement message are transmitted correctly.

The controller will stop trying communicate with this device after a certain amount of time, which depends on the size and complexity of the network. The controller will mark the device as failed and ignore any further communication request to this link unless receiving an unsolicited message from this failed device.

The worst-case scenario is that the device is only reachable occasionally since this will always motivate the controller to try as hard as he can to reach the device that again causes a lot of traffic and delay for other command executions.

Certain Z-Wave network management tools even allow users to access these routing tables to see how the different

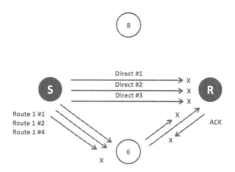

Figure 2.26.: Multiple communication attempts in Z-Wave-step 2

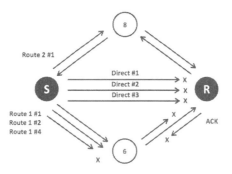

Figure 2.27.: Multiple communication attempts in Z-Wave-step 3

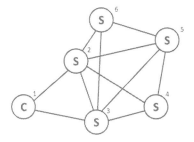

Figure 2.28.: Example of a meshed network

nodes in the network can communicate with each other.

Figure 2.28 shows an example of a meshed network with one controller and five other nodes. The controller as primary controller has Node Id 1. It can communicate directly with node 2 and 3. There is no direct connection from node 1 to node 4, 5 and 6. A routing table for example network is presented in Figure 2.29.

The rows of the table contain the source nodes and the columns contain the destination nodes. A **1** in a cell indicates that the two nodes are direct neighbors.

The example given in Figure 2.30 shall explain the connection between source node 1 and destination node 4. The cell between node 1 and 4 is marked **0**. This means the two nodes are not neighbors and cannot communicate directly. The route goes via node 3 that is in direct range both from node 1 and node 4. This results in two valid routes between node 1 and node 4:

- $1 \rightarrow 3 \rightarrow 4$ or

- $1 \rightarrow 2 \rightarrow 4$.

| Source Nodes | to 1 | to 2 | to 3 | to 4 | to 5 | to 6 |
|---|---|---|---|---|---|---|
| Source Node 1 | (white) | (grey) | (grey) | (black) | (black) | (black) |
| Source Node 2 | (grey) | (white) | (grey) | (grey) | (grey) | (grey) |
| Source Node 3 | (grey) | (grey) | (white) | (grey) | (grey) | (grey) |
| Source Node 4 | (black) | (grey) | (grey) | (white) | (grey) | (black) |
| Source Node 5 | (black) | (grey) | (grey) | (grey) | (white) | (grey) |
| Source Node 6 | (black) | (grey) | (grey) | (black) | (grey) | (white) |

Black box: 0
Grey box: 1

Figure 2.29.: Routing Table for Example network

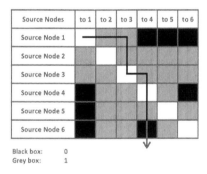

Black box: 0
Grey box: 1

Figure 2.30.: Routing from Node 1 via Node 3 to Node 4

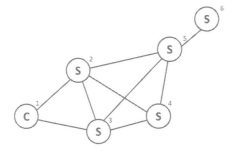

Figure 2.31.: Example of meshed network with one distant
node

In the next example shown in Figure 2.31 node 6 can only communicate with the rest of the network using node 5 as repeater. Since the controller does not have a direct connection to node 5, the controller needs to use one of the following routes:

- $1 \rightarrow 3 \rightarrow 4 \rightarrow 5 \rightarrow 6$ or

- $1 \rightarrow 2 \rightarrow 5 \rightarrow 6$.

The routing table for this example is presented in Figure 2.32.

A controller will always try first to transmit its message directly to the destination. If this is not possible, it will use its routing table to find the next best way to the destination. The controller can select up to three alternative routes and will try to send the message via these routes. Only if all three routes fail (the controller does not receive an acknowledgement from the destination), the controller will report a

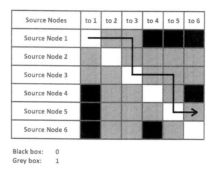

| Source Nodes | to 1 | to 2 | to 3 | to 4 | to 5 | to 6 |
|---|---|---|---|---|---|---|
| Source Node 1 | | | | | | |
| Source Node 2 | | | | | | |
| Source Node 3 | | | | | | |
| Source Node 4 | | | | | | |
| Source Node 5 | | | | | | |
| Source Node 6 | | | | | | |

Black box:  0
Grey box:  1

Figure 2.32.: Routing table for Example with one distant
node

failure. If one alternative route works, the controller will try
this route first the next time to save time to find a proper
route. Only if this previously successful route fails again,
will the controller try to find a next route.

To summarize this communication behavior:

1. A successful communication only happens if a sender
   receives a conformation or acknowledgement from the
   destination node that its data message was received
   correctly.

2. If this fails within a certain time, the sender tries two
   more times using the same route.

3. If this still fails, the sender will try two more alternating routes, again with three communication attempts
   per route.

4. If all up to nine communications failed, the controller
   will report a communication failure.

# 2.8. Device and Network Types

## 2.8.1. Controller and Slaves

The previous chapter already mentioned the existence of two different device types:

- Controllers and

- Slaves.

The most obvious difference between controller and slave is the ability to build and manage a network. This is only possible with a controller. The controller that is used to include new nodes into the network by assigning its Home ID and providing a Node ID is referred to as the Primary Controller. All other controllers are called Secondary Controllers Controllers are further differentiated according to their mobility.

- Portable Controllers are battery operated and can be moved around

- Static Controllers are mains powered and they are installed on a fixed location

Another differentiation between node types comes from the way a node handles routing information resp. stores information about the structure of the network. The knowledge about the network and the different routes to other nodes determines the communication abilities of the different nodes. Here Z-Wave distinguishes between normal slaves and routing slaves. Table 2.8 shows the different node types

|  | Neighbors | Route | Possible functions |
|---|---|---|---|
| Controller | Knows all neighbors | Has access to the complete routing table | Can communicate with every device in the network, if a route exists. |
| Slave | Knows all neighbors | Has no information about the routing table | Can only reply to the node that he has received the message from. Hence, can not send unsolicited messages |
| Routing Slave | Knows all his neighbors | Has partial knowledge about the routing table | Can reply to the node that he has received the message from and can send unsolicited messages to a number of predefined nodes he has a route to. |

Table 2.8.: Properties of the Z-Wave device models

with their knowledge about the network and subsequently their communication abilities:

From this comparison a number of basic rules arises:

- Every Z-Wave device can receive and acknowledge messages.

- Controllers can send messages to all nodes in the network, solicited and unsolicited (*The master can talk whenever he wants and to whom he wants.*).

- Slaves cannot send unsolicited messages but only answer to requests (*The slave shall only speak when he is asked.*).

- Routing slaves can answer requests and they are allowed to send unsolicited messages to certain nodes the controller has predefined (*The sensor slave is still a slave but - on permission - he may speak up.*). [4]

---

[4] Routing Slave is a misleading term because it suggests that this

| Device Type | Application |
|---|---|
| Slave | Only fixed installed mains powered devices like wall switches, wall dimmers or Venetian blind controllers, you can have battery operated slaves that are FLiRs |
| Routing Slave | Battery-operated devices and mobile applicable devices as for example sensors with battery operation, wall plugs for Schuko and plug types, thermostats and heaters with battery operation and all other slave applications, meanwhile all new devices including fixed installation wall devices are routing slaves. |

Table 2.9.: Typical applications for slaves

Since the functionality of standard slaves is quite limited, this type of node is only used for dimmers and switches that are installed in a fixed location. Every kind of sensor or any device that can be used on multiple locations must be a routing slave or even a controller because he may be required to send out certain information.

Typical applications for slaves are shown in Table 2.9.

## 2.8.2. Mains and battery-operated devices

The way a node is powered greatly determines its ability to communicate. A node that has plenty of energy can stay awake with its receiver turned on and immediately react to all messages sent to this node. In case where a node is powered by a battery or even with energy harvesting technology energy saving is critical. Such a device needs to be in deep sleep state or even turned off most of the time and

device is routing messages. All Z-Wave devices that are mains powered can and will route messages. The specific function of the routing slave is the ability to store several routes to destinations and therefore the ability to send unsolicited messages.

can therefore not easily be reached by other nodes.

In a Z-Wave network there are four different types of devices defined by the way they handle the energy and their capabilities to communicate:

## 2.8.3. Mains Powered Devices

A mains powered device is always awake and can therefore always receive messages and answer them. This capability allows mains powered devices to act as repeaters in a Z-Wave network.

Remember: Only mains powered devices can act as repeaters in a Z-Wave network.

## 2.8.4. Battery-Operated Devices

The main objective of a battery-operated device is to preserve the battery power and only use as much battery power as needed. Battery-powered devices are therefore in a deep-sleep state most of the time. In deep-sleep state they are not able to communicate with other devices.

In order to communicate with other devices the battery-operated device needs to be woken up and sent to sleep mode right after communication takes place. To maintain a minimal level of responsiveness and to provide for configuration messages from time to time and to use battery-operated devices Z-Wave offers three basic solutions:

1. Devices with wakeup intervals

2. Frequently listening battery devices

3. Devices with manual wakeup

## 2.8.5. Wakeup Interval

Devices with wakeup interval will wakeup after a defined
interval and send out a wakeup notification to a node that
keeps track of this device (typically the controller). Other
devices are able to communicate with this device and send
out messages to this device (The controller know about
the status of the battery operated device and will queue
messages in a waiting queue.). After all communication is
done the controller is supposed to send the device back into
deep sleep state. If no communication happens the battery-
operated device will go back into deep sleep state mode after
a defined time (typically some seconds up to one minute).
The simple fact that a battery operated device with wakeup
interval needs to announce its wakeup event requires that
such a device is a routing slave.

## 2.8.6. FLIRS - Frequently Listening Routing Slaves

The FLIRS device is an interesting concept to allow battery-
operated devices an immediate reaction to commands. The
idea is that a battery operated device wakes up periodically
for a very short period of time and listens if there is any message to receive. If this is not the case, the device goes back
to sleep mode right away. The wakeup period for FLIRS
device is either 250 ms or 1 sec.

In order to "catch" a FLIRS device during a very short
wakeup the sending device needs to send a so-called wakeup
beam for at least the wakeup time period. This wakeup
beam has a special pattern the FLIRS device can receive

and knows that it is supposed to stay awake for further communication.

The very short periodical wakeup allows operating such a device with batteries for more than one year depending on the application and the energy needed for other actions of the device.

Typical FLIRS devices are door locks or sirens that need to act immediately on a signal but still need the freedom to be placed in a location independent of mains connection.

From the controller point of view FLIRS devices will act like normal mains powered devices. They will answer messages within a reasonable time period of 250 ms resp. 1 sec. However, to preserve battery lifetime FLIRS devices don't route messages.

### 2.8.7. Devices with manual wakeup

Remote controls that are battery-operated do not wake up regularly but only when button is pressed. This means that a device with manual wakeup is unreachable for a controller unless there is some manual interaction by the user.

# 2.9. Communication behavior of different node types

Table 2.10 shows what kind of Z-Wave node type combinations are possible.

| Device Type | Controller | Routing Slave | Slave |
|---|---|---|---|
| Mains | yes, called static controller | yes | yes |
| Battery / wakeup interval | unlikely | yes | no |
| FLIRS | unlikely | yes | possible but rare |
| Manual wakeup | yes, portable controllers | possible but rare | no |

Table 2.10.: Possible combinations of node types

## 2.9.1. Exclusion

The exclusion of a device is reverting the actions performed for inclusion. The Home ID of the network needs to be deleted in the device and all information of this device need to be deleted from the routing tables of the network.

The normal way to exclude a device is to perform an **exclusion process**. In most cases this is similar to the inclusion process. The excluded device needs to confirm the exclusion. It means the device to be excluded needs to be present in the network. The primary controller will send an exclusion request to the device and this device needs to agree to the exclusion by confirming that the old Home Id was successfully deleted. Typically there is a manual interaction needed on the device to confirm the exclusion. This confirmation of the device is needed for the primary controller to update its routing table.

**Security aspects of inclusion and exclusion**   Both operations require a manual action on the device so physical
access to the advice is required. A controller needs to send
out an information that it will include/exclude and the device itself will answer depending on a manual interaction,
typically pushing a button. This will ensure that only devices that are in physical possession of the owner can be
excluded or included.

There is one exception to this rule. Modern Z-Wave devices may support a so-called **auto-inclusion**. This means
that in case they are not belonging to one network already
they wait for the first controller announcing its willingness
to include the device and will agree to this inclusion. On
one hand this greatly simplifies the building of Z-Wave networks but on the other hand this also implies a great risk
that a different controller is the first asking the fresh and
new device to be included.

The legal owner of the device has however always the
chance to exclude the device from the network since he is in
physical possession of the device. Exclusion can therefore
be done

- from any controller issuing an exclusion request,

- if and only if there is a manual confirmation on the
  device.

## 2.9.2. Failed Node List

The routing table in the primary controller always shows the actual status of the network after inclusion of the devices. During normal operation a node can however

- go out of operation (damaged) or

- can be moved to a different location.

In both cases the routing table is not longer valid and communication to the moved or damaged node may fail (if the node is just moved its possible that it was moved luckily in direct range of the controller or into a place where his old neighbors can still reach him).

Any failed communication to a node results in an error message. In parallel the controller will mark this node as failed node by putting him into a so-called **failed node list**. The failed node list contains nodes with a failed communication. Being in the failed node list does not necessarily mean that node is permanently gone. Any working communication will move the node back into the original routing table.

If no successful communication happens, the node will stay in the failed node list and can be removed from the network without any corporation of the failed node.

The reason for this is obvious. Failed nodes can no longer communicate their agreement to the exclusion.

In order to force a node out of the network certain requirements need to be made:

1. The node needs to be in the failed node list.

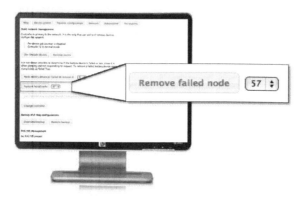

Figure 2.33.: Screenshot of a Z-Wave Controller with a button to exclude a failed node

2. The controller needs to receive a command from the user to force the node out of the network. The controller will never automatically perform such an action.

3. After the command to force out a node the controller will do a very last attempt to reach this node and will only execute the exclusion if this last attempt fails as well.

Figure 2.33 shows a user dialog to enable to remove a failed node from the network.

Battery-operated devices with wakeup interval or manual wakeup will never enter into the failed node list since the controller knows that it is not possible to just send them messages. Since there are plenty of reasons why these

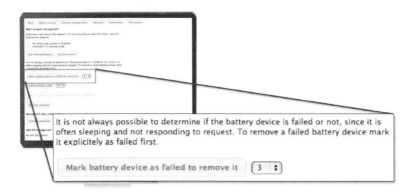

Figure 2.34.: Screenshot of a Z-Wave Controller that allows to mark nodes as failed

battery-operated devices may not announce their wakeup to the controller - e.g. no button is pressed on a remote control for some time  the controller cannot just assume they are gone.

The main function of the failed node list is to exclude devices from further routing attempts. Since battery operated devices don't route at all, there is no pressing need to remove them from the network. Some Z-Wave controllers however allow to move battery operated devices manually into the failed node list in order to exclude them in a second step  just for cosmetic reasons- Figure 2.34 shows an example of such a user dialog.

### 2.9.3. Routing table update of controllers and routing slaves

As long as there is just one controller in the network this very controller is managing the routing table and is immediately informed about any change of the network caused by inclusion or exclusion.

Z-Wave allows operating multiple controllers in one network. Still there is one central instance keeping track of the network configuration referred to as the primary controller but the other controllers - in Z-Wave referred to as **secondary controller** still have their own configuration of the network that may become invalid.

The primary controller therefore needs to periodically update all other controllers and the routing slaves about changes of the configuration.

The challenge arises from the fact that some to these devices are battery-operated and therefore hard or impossible to reach. Communication problems in Z-Wave networks may therefore simply come from the fact that a battery operated device tries to reach a node that no longer exists. The next chapter will show different ways to overcome this problem.

# 2.10. Auto-(Re)-Configuration of Networks

The process to update the controller(s) about the new status of the network including all routing information in all devices is called network rediscovery. Some software may also call it **network redetection** or **network repair**.

In all cases the following functions are performed:

1. The primary controller will ask all known nodes to rediscover their neighbors and to report an updated list of neighbors back to the controller.

2. Depending on the implementation the controller may inform all other controllers about the new status and update their routing tables as well.

3. Depending on the implementation the controller will also update all routing slaves about changed routes.

Depending on the size of the network this rediscovery process may take some time and create a lot of network traffic. This operation will therefore not be executed automatically by the controller but on user command only. Certain software solutions allow to setup a periodic network rediscovery, typically at night time, when the high traffic does not interfere with user interactions. A special challenge comes from battery-operated devices that may need to be updated. The controller will have to wait for the next wakeup of these devices and in case of portable controllers, that only wakeup when manually operated, this may take a long time.

Figure 2.35 shows an example of a user dialog for performing a network rediscovery.

The next two chapters explain methods the network can apply to solve routing and communication problems without further interaction by the user.

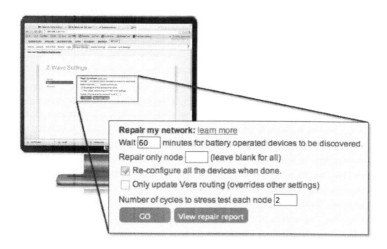

Figure 2.35.: Network Rediscovery

## 2.10.1. Explorer Frame

The explorer frame is a powerful tool to overcome communication problems in a network caused by incorrect network and routing information.

The explorer frame is a special frame that is sent out as a broadcast and is routed forward by every node in the network supporting the explorer frame process. This process is sometimes refered to as flooding. Of course there needs to be a pruning mechanism to stop the forwarding to make sure the network does not get overloaded with repeatedly forwarded and broadcasted messages.

The explorer frame has a source address and a destination address. Every node forwarding the explorer frame adds its own Node ID to the frame. If there is at least one valid route from the sender to its desired destination, one explorer frame will eventually reach this destination now carrying all the routing nodes used on its way. This information is the new and also the best route from the given source to the given destination. The receiver is then supposed to send the explorer frame information back to the sender using the route just detected. The sender receives this very valuable information and can update its routing table accordingly. Because the explorer frame is generating a lot of network traffic, it is only used as the last resort after all other communication attempts fail. On the other hand the explorer frame technology will find always a valid way if there is a valid way.

## 2.10.2. Rediscovery using special controller functions

Prior to the introduction of explorer frames Z-Wave used a more complicated but still valid process to make sure the Z-Wave network is working stable and can handle changes in the configuration automatically.

### Static Update-Controller (SUC)

The Static Update Controller (SUC) is a special function of a static controller. Most static controllers (a controller with fixed location and powered by mains) can perform as a SUC. However, the function typically needs to be activated first.

**The SUC acts as a known central entity** that always has the latest and therefore most valid routing table of the network.

For all other devices in the network there is the rule: **When in doubt ask the SUC.**

In order to play the role of the central entity to inform all others about the latest status of the network

- the SUCs Node ID needs to be known by all nodes in the network,

- all changes of the network must at a minimum be reported to the SUC,

- all nodes that store routes (controllers and routing slaves) must have a valid route to the SUC to ask for updates when needed and

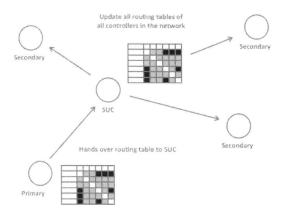

Figure 2.36.: SUC in a Z-Wave Network

- the SUC needs to be awake and ready to answer questions all the time.

The last requirement limits the SUC function to static controllers that are mains powered and always awake and always in the same physical location. No portable device or battery operated device can act as SUC.

Figure 2.36 shows a network with a SUC present that is informing all other devices about changes in the routing table and the configuration of the network.

Having an active SUC in the network allows the user to keep the primary controller role on a portable controller. Every change of the network caused by inclusion or exclusion of a node by the primary controller will be reported to the SUC and is then available to all other controllers, even if the primary controller is not active (see Figure 2.37).

105

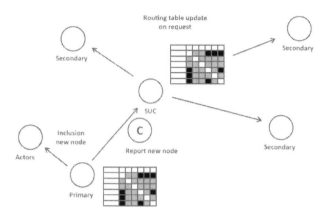

Figure 2.37.: Update of the Routing table in a SUC

Since controllers are typically battery-operated (e.g. battery operated wall controllers) and therefore not active all the time, these controllers have to request an updated routing table periodically or at least when woken up by pressing a button. To perform this task the mobile battery-operated controllers need to be informed about the presence of a SUC in the network.

If the original mobile battery-operated primary controller is lost or damaged, the SUC can assign the primary privilege to a new mobile controller, protecting the user from re-establishing the whole network with a brand new primary controller and having a different Home ID.

**Static Id Server (SIS)**

The idea of the SIS (Static Id Server) is to allow multiple controllers to include devices. This is very convenient, particularly in larger networks and particularly in a network with multiple remote controls. The update function of new devices in the routing table is already solved by the SUC. The only remaining problem to overcome when using multiple controllers to include new devices is the maintenance of the Node Ids. There needs to be one central instance that keeps track of issued and available Node Ids. The SIS plays that very role.

The SIS acts as depot for new Node Ids which can be assigned by mobile controllers. Having an SIS present in the network allows every controller in the network to include further devices. The including controller first requests a new Node Id from the SIS and then assigns this new Node Id to the device being included. The SIS makes sure that two nodes never get assigned the same Node Id. A model of a SIS server in a Z-Wave-Network is presented in Figure 2.38.

With the presence of a SUC and a SIS the role of the primary controller as the single instance to make network changes becomes irrelevant. The primary controller will still remain a primary controller but its rights and duties have been moved to the SUC and the SIS.

A network with SUC/SIS support has its advantages and disadvantages:

**Advantages:**

- The actual network topology and the information about all nodes is saved in a mains powered static controller

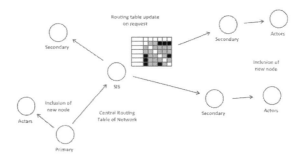

Figure 2.38.: SIS Server in a Z-Wave-Network

and are therefore better protected than within a mobile battery powered device.

- All controllers in a network can include and exclude devices.

- The network configuration and handling becomes very flexible.

## Disadvantages:

- An inclusion controller can only include devices if it has a wireless connection to the SIS.

- With the SIS there exists a "Single Point of Failure". A damaged SIS results in a complete new network setup.

Since the SUC/SIS functionality is already included in the firmware of most modern static controllers such as gateways

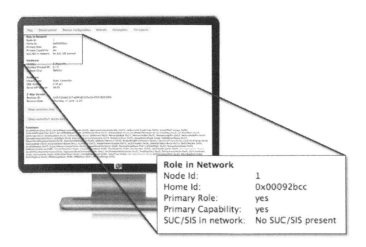

| Role in Network | |
| --- | --- |
| Node Id: | 1 |
| Home Id: | 0x00092bcc |
| Primary Role: | yes |
| Primary Capability: | yes |
| SUC/SIS in network: | No SUC/SIS present |

Figure 2.39.: Controller rules shown in a Gateway User Interface

or USB dongles, most Z-Wave networks implement SUC and SIS functions.

A static controller can also be a primary controller, as well as it can have SUC/SIS functionality. This configuration is typical in most Z-Wave networks today .

Figure 2.39 represents the controller rules in a gateway user interface.

## 2.10.3. Explorer Frames versus SUC/SIS in one network

Explorer Frames and the SUC/SIS architecture can work in parallel in a network. Since Explorer Frames are a fairly recent addition to the Z-Wave protocol devices with Explorer Frame support typically also support SUC/SIS. However, older devices with SUC/SIS support may not support Explorer Frames. If both approaches are supported, the network will automatically choose the option that is appropriate and able to handle the problem. The main difference between the two approaches can be summarized like:

- **Explorer Frames will always find a valid way in the network without any further help by users as long as there is a way.**

- **SUC/SIC helps devices to find a way but there are some actions to be done in order to make this help effective. Nevertheless, certain limits to this help still apply.**

The limit in a SUC/SIS architecture without Explorer Frames are:

1. Inclusion and Exclusion must be done in *'direct range'*. These two commands require that the controller and the device to be excluded or included must be in direct wireless range. A SIS in the network allows every controller in the network to include and exlude devices, nevertheless, the controller performing the action must be in *'direct range'* too.

2. Whenever there is a change in the network either adding devices, removing devices or moving devices (this does not apply to portable controllers that were designed to be portable), a network rediscovery is needed.

3. A special challenge are battery-operated devices because they will not be found during a network rediscovery, simply because they are in deep sleep state. The common option is to keep the network rediscovery process open for a much longer time than required and hope that the battery-operated device will wakeup during this time to identify themselves with their new position in the network. Figure 2.40 shows that users are typically required to set a deadline for this waiting time (*Wait xx minutes for battery operated devices to be discovered*). It is obvious that this is a tradeoff between the time the network is busy rediscovering and the chance to 'find' the battery-operated device awake and - depending on the wakeup interval - the chance is not 100 % that the waiting is worth doing.

**How many devices need to support Explorer Frames in a network?**

It is possible to mix devices with and without Explorer Frame in one network. Regardless of the number of Explorer-Frame-Devices the SUC/SIS function will always work **if there is at least one static controller** in the network that will then act as SUC/SIS.

> Hint: Due to memory constraints in the Z-Wave chip it is possible that certain Z-Wave controllers support either Explorer Frames or support SUC/SIS functionality but not both.

In order to make Explorer Frames applicable the following requirements need to be met:

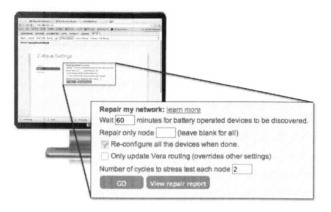

Figure 2.40.: Network rediscovery user interface with special handling for batter-operated devices

1. The primary controller must support Explorer Frames.

2. The device that shall be included or excluded or moved needs to support Explorer Frames.

3. If (1) and (2) are not in direct range, there must be at least one route only using devices with Explorer Frame Support.

For a user or even for an installer it may be difficult to find out if all three requirements are met. It is therefore strongly recommended to use as many Explorer-Frame capable devices as possible.

**How to know if a device supports Explorer Frames?**

Unless the manual mentions support for Explorer Frames the firmware version of the device needs to be checked. The Pepper One Device Database mentioned in Appendix C gives information about the firmware version used. This information is also available in the products section at www.z-wavealliance.org in the PIC statement that is provided for every Z-Wave certified device.

Device Firmware are built using a SDK (Systems Development Kit) provided by Sigma Designs. The following SDK versions support Explorer Frames:

- Every SDK Version 6.0 and up

- All SDKs between Version 4.5 and 4.9

Table 2.11 summarizes the user actions needed and therefore the 'convenience level' of the different way to rediscover a Z-Wave network. Clearly only networks with complete Explorer Frame support are truly plug'n play.

# 2.11. Network configurations

## 2.11.1. Z-Wave Network with one portable controller

Z-Wave works by starting with a very small network and extending this network later on as needed. A typical small network consists of a remote control and a couple of switches or dimmers. The remote control acts as the primary controller and both includes and controls the switches and dimmers. Before inclusion the dimmers and switches should be

| Action | no SUC/SIS | SUC/SIS | Explorer Frames |
|---|---|---|---|
| Inclusion and Exclusion | primary controller must be in direct range | a controller must be in direct range | **no limitations**, device can be everywhere and inclusion is done by primary controller and routing |
| Mains powered device moves in network | Network reconfiguration mandatory plus updating of all routes in the network that are impacted by the node moved | Network reconfirmation required to update SUC, other update will happen automatically | **no user action needed** |
| Battery powered slave device moves in network | not supported | may be healed under certain circumstances | **no user action required** |
| Multiple Controllers in Network | users need to make sure that controllers are all update, action required after all change in network | **no user action required** | **no user action required** |

Table 2.11.: Comparison of different Z-Wave network management modes

installed in their final location to make sure that a correct list of neighbors will be recognized and reported. Figure 2.41 shows a Z-Wave Network with one portable controller.

A network configuration like this works well as long as the remote control can reach all switches and dimmers directly (the node which is to be controlled is in range). In case the controlled node is not in range, the user may experience delays, because the remote control needs to detect the network structure and calculate a route first before controlling the device. In case a device was included and moved afterwards to a new position, this particular device can only be controlled by the remote control if it is in direct range. Otherwise the communication will fail, because the routing table entry for this particular device is wrong and only few remote controls are able to do a network rediscovery.

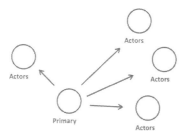

Figure 2.41.: Z-Wave Network with one portable controller

## 2.11.2. Z-Wave Network with one static controller

Another typical network consists of a static controller (see Figure 2.42) - mostly PC software plus Z-Wave transceiver as a USB dongle or an IP gateway as well as a number of switches and dimmers.

The static controller is the primary controller and includes all other devices. Because a static controller is bound to a certain location, the other Z-Wave devices must be included while being in direct range with the static controller. They will typically be installed at their final location after inclusion.

## 2.11.3. Networks with multiple controllers

In a larger network several controllers will work together. A static controller e.g. a PC is used for the configuration and management of the system and one or several remote controls carry out certain functions in different places.

115

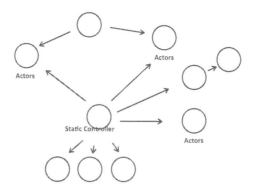

Figure 2.42.: Example of a network with one static controller

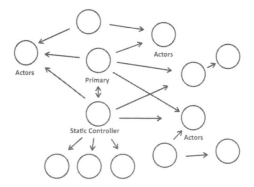

Figure 2.43.: Z-Wave Network with multiple controllers

If a network has multiple controllers (as shown in Figure 2.43), the user needs to determine which of the controllers will be the primary controller.

As long as there is at least one static controller, this static controller will become SUC and SIS and subsequently manage the network very well.

If the network only consists of a series of portable controllers, the challenge of the synchronization of the different controllers routing table remains unsolved. In this case there should be at least one static controller added in a SUC role to stabilize the network. If all devices support Explorer Frames this is not necessary.

# 3. Z-Wave Application Layer

So far we have only looked at how different nodes can communicate with each other. The application layer of the Z-Wave product now defines and specifies **what and why** two nodes communicate with each other.

## 3.1. Devices and Commands

### 3.1.1. Types of Z-Wave Devices

In theory every controllable or controlling device in a home or office can be equipped with Z-Wave technology. Hence one should expect a broad variety of different devices and functions. However, there are some basic functionality patterns that allow categorizing different devices.

Each device will either control other devices or being controlled by other devices. In the Z-Wave terminology controlling devices are called **controllers**, reporting devices are called **sensors** and controlled devices are called **actors or actuators**. It is also possible to combine a logical sensor controller or actor function within one physical device. Figure 3.1 shows the three basic device types.

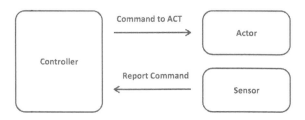

Figure 3.1.: Z-Wave Controllers, Sensors and Actors

Actors switch either digital (on / off for an electrical switch) or analogue signals (0% ... 100% for a dimmer or window blind control). Sensors deliver either a digital signal (door, glass breaking, motion detector, window button on the wall) or an analogue signal (temperature, humidity, power).

In today's market of Z-Wave device there is a surprisingly short list of different product categories. Nearly all Z-Wave devices on the market can be categorized into one of the following function groups:

1. Electrical switches are designed either as plug-in modules for wall outlets or as replacements for traditional wall switches (digital actors). Its also possible to have these actors already built into certain electrical appliances such as electrical stoves or heaters.

2. Electrical dimmers, either as plug-in modules for wall outlets or as replacements for traditional wall dimmers (analogue actors)

3. Motor control, usually to open or close a door, a window, a window sun blind or a venetian blind (analogue or digital actors)

4. Electrical Displays or other kind of signal emission such as siren, Led panel, etc. (digital actors)

5. Sensors of different kind to measure parameters like temperature, humidity, gas concentration (e.g. carbon dioxide or carbon monoxide) (analogue or digital sensors)

6. Thermostat controls: either as a one knob control or using a temperature display (analogue sensors)

7. Thermostats controls such as TRVs (Thermostat Radiator Valves) or floor heating controls (analogue or digital actors)

8. Remote Controls either as universal remote control with IR support or as dedicated Z-Wave Remote Control with special keys for network functions, group and/or scene control

9. USB sticks and IP gateways to allow PC software to access Z-Wave networks. Using IP communication these interfaces also allow remote access over the internet

10. Door locks of various kinds

## 3.1.2. Command Classes

Every message that is exchanged between Z-Wave devices is called a command. Commands can be classified into three major categories:

- ask a device to do something (`Set`)

- ask a device to provide something (`Get`)

- report a certain value or status to a device (`Report`)

According to the different device types the `Set`, `Get` and `Report` commands may mean different things and need to be specified further.

Z-Wave organizes all the commands in so called **Command Classes**. Command classes describe a certain function of a device and group all necessary commands to deal with this function.

### Example 1  the battery function

If a device wants to deal with the battery function of another device there is no clear meaning of a `Set` command, since there is nothing to set for a remote battery. Clearly a `Get` command makes sense since there may be a need to ask for a battery status value or the actual battery drain current. Since these values need to be reported the `Report` command is required as well.

This pretty much describes a Z-Wave command class called `Battery`.

The battery command class knows two commands:

- `Get()` ... ask a device to report its actual status

- `Report()` ... the actual charging status is reported.

The different functions of different device require a long list of command classes that reach from lighting control via heating to door locks and beyond.

## Example 2 a simple switch

A normal on/off switch is referred to as a binary switch. The basic function of a binary switch is to be switched on and off. With a Z-Wave system it is also possible to know the status of the switch, hence a status request function and a status report function is required too.

- `Set(value)`: is sent from a controller to the switch to turn the switch on or off

- `Get()`: is sent from the controller to the switch to request a report about the switching state

- `Report()`: is sent from the switch back to the controller as a response to the Binary Switch Get Command

These three commands and responses are grouped and referred to as command class `Binary Switch`. If a certain Z-Wave device supports the command class `Binary Switch` it is supposed to be able to deal with all these commands:

- The switch needs to understand the set command and set the switch accordingly.

- The switch is able to receive a get command and is able to response with a report command in the proper format.

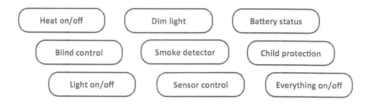

Figure 3.2.: Examples of different command classes

Figure 3.2 shows a sub set of Z-Wave command classes. Most but not all of them support one or more of the basic commands `Set`, `Get` and `Report` and other more specific commands.

## Example 3 a dimmer

A dimming function can certainly be realized by the three basic functions `Set`, `Get` and `Report`. `Set` will allow to set a dimmer level, `Get` asks for the actual dimming level and `Report` sends the actual dimming level.

However, there is also a need for a command to start the dimming process and to stop the dimming process to emulate the behaviour of a normal wall switch. Hence the command class `Multilevel Switch`, that controls a dimmer has two additional commands `DIMSTART(direction)` and `DIMSTOP()`.

Command classes are identified by a single byte number. Annex B shows the list of command classes with their ID number and the commands.

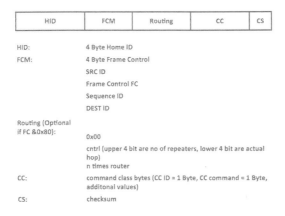

Figure 3.3.: Frame Layout for Command Classes

The commands within the command class are identified by a single byte number as well. This leads to the a command class layout as shown in Figure 3.3.

In case there are no further values to transmit, the smallest possible command class has a length of 2 bytes. Most of commands however are larger in size.

### 3.1.3. Command Class Basic

There is one very special command class called **Basic** (see Figure 3.4). **Basic** is a kind of wildcard command classes. It is not tied to a special device function but just implements the very basic of commands:

- **Set:** set a value between 0 and 255 (0x00 0xff);

- **Get:** ask the device to report a value;

125

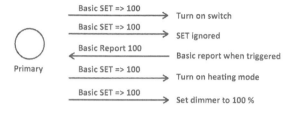

Figure 3.4.: **Basic** Command Class

- **Report**: response to the Get command. Reports a value between 0 and 255 (0x00 0xff).

The specialty of the **Basic** command class is that every device will interpret the basic commands dependent of its specific functionality:

- A binary switch will switch on when receiving a value 255 and switch off when receiving a value of 0;

- A thermostat may turn into a convenience temperature mode when receiving value = 0 and may turn into a energy saving mode when receiving a higher value;

- A temperature sensor will issue a basic report and send a integer temperature value;

- A door sensor will either send out a value = 0 in case the door is closed or a 255 (0xff) when the door is opened.

The basic command class is the smallest common denominator of all Z-Wave devices. Every Z-Wave device must support the `Basic` command class, however certain commands may be ignored if there is no meaningful implementation in the device.

## 3.1.4. Device Classes

To allow interoperability between different Z-Wave devices from different manufacturers, certain Z-Wave devices must have certain well-defined functions above and beyond the basic command class. The structure behind these requirements is called a device class. A device class refers to certain device types and defines which command classes are mandatory to support.

There are three levels of device class specifications:

- Every device must belong to a **basic device class**.

- Devices can be further specified by assigning them to a **generic device class**.

- Further functionality can be defined as assigning the device to a **specific device class**.

### Basic Device Class

The basic device class makes a distinction merely whether the device is a controller, a Slave or a Routing-Slave. Therefore every device belongs to one basic device class.

## Generic Device Class

The generic device class defines the basic function a device is supposed to offer as a controller or slave. A list of device classes is available in Annex A .

## Specific Device Class

Assigning a specific device class to a Z-Wave device allows to further specify the functionality of the device. Assigning a specific device class is voluntary and only makes sense, if the device really supports all specific functions of a specific device class. Special device classes are, for example:

- Setback Thermostat (`SETBACK THERMOSTAT`) is a specific device class of the generic device class `Thermostat`;

- Multi-level Power Switch (`MULTILEVEL POWER SWITCH`) is a specific device class of the generic device class `MULTILEVEL SWITCH`.

Once a Z-Wave device is assigned to a specific device class, it is required to support a set of command classes as functions of this specific device class. These required command classes are called **mandatory command classes** and they are comprised of certain generic and specific device classes. Above and beyond the mandatory device classes, Z-Wave devices can support further **optional command classes**. These optional command classes may be very useful but the standard does not enforce the implementation of them. A Z-Wave manufacturer is allowed to implement an unlimited number of optional device classes, however if these device classes are implemented, the standard defines how these

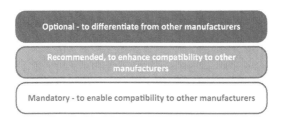

Figure 3.5.: Optionally, recommended and mandatory Command Classes within a device class

commands and functions are to be supported. The recommended and mandatory Command Classes within a device class can be seen in Figure 3.5.

The basic device class, the generic and, if available, the specific device class are announced by the device during inclusion, using a **Node Information Frame** (for more information about Node Information Frame please refer to 3.2.1). As well as the device classes, the Node Information Frame also announces all optional command classes of the device included. With this announcement, a controller can control and use an included Z-Wave device according to its functionality. Figure 3.6 shows the different implementation of a Device Class Binary Power Switch by different vendors.

A Z-Wave device works according to the Z-Wave standard if

- It belongs to a basic device class and a generic device class and is able to report these classes on request using a Node Information Frame.

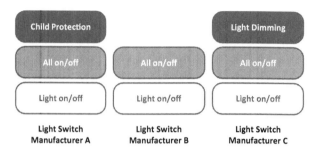

Figure 3.6.: Different Implementation of a Device Class Binary Power Switch by different vendors

- It supports all mandatory command classes of the basic and generic command class by sending commands and reports as well as accepting and executing commands according specification of the command class.

- In case a specific device class is defined, the **mandatory command classes** of this specific device class need to be supported as well and the specific device class needs to be reported on request.

- In case optional command classes are implemented, these command classes need to be announced in the Node Information Frame on request and need to be supported according to the Z-Wave command class specifications.

Z-Wave defines a broad variety of command classes covering almost every aspect of home automation and control.

Figure 3.7.: Wall Plug

Nevertheless, it is possible that manufacturers want to implement further functionality not already defined in a command class specification.

The command class `proprietary function` is defined to cover these needs. A proprietary function would allow a manufacturer to implement specific functions that can then be used only by other devices supporting this proprietary function as well.

The use of a proprietary function is subject to approval by the Z-Wave Alliance certification authority and is required to be documented extensively. So far only very few devices make use of this function. Typically new requirements result sooner or later in an amendment to the existing standard, which makes this function part of the official standard and any proprietary extension becomes obsolete.

One example shall illustrate the use of device classes and command classes:

**Example: Definition of a Wall Plug**

131

A manufacturer wants to offer a plug-in switch as shown in Figure 3.7. The basic function of this switch is switching the power on and off. Since such a device can be used at multiple locations, the basic device class `routing slave` is used. As a binary switch the device belongs into the generic device class `Binary Switch`. It is allowed and in this case even recommended to use a specific device class `Binary Power Switch` since this Schuko plug-in switch will always switch power lines.

- Basis class: `Routing-Slave`

- Generic class: `Binary Switch`

- Special class: `Binary Power Switch`

1. The `Binary Switch` device class requires the implementation of the mandatory command class `binary switch` and of course the implementation of the `Basic` command class.

2. As binary power switch the device is furthermore requested to implement the so-called `switch all` command class. This command classes defines the reaction of a device when receiving a `switch all` command that can be sent from a controller to all devices in the network. (The purpose of this command is to quickly shut down or bring up all electrical loads in a home.) The `switch all` command class allows to

define under which circumstances a device
should react to this `switch all` command
issued by the controller. A generic switch is
not required to implement such a command
class but ignore the `switch all` command,
since an `all off` command may not mean
something useful to a generic switch. In
case of a power switch an `all off` command is clearly defined and therefore a mandatory command class.

It is allowed by the standard not to implement
the `switch all` command class but in this case
the device is not allowed to announce a specific
device class `Binary Power Switch`. A switching device without `switch all` support which
just announces a generic device class `binary switch`
would still be a valid Z-Wave compliant device.

- The manufacturer wants to offer more a
  competitive product and adds further functionality to the switching device. One may
  be the so called child protection command
  class. A child protection function on a binary switch means the ability to disable local control capability and only allow switching the device wirelessly.

- If the manufacturer decides to implement
  such function the standard defines in the
  `Protection` command class how to do this.
  Also the optional command class `Protection`
  needs to be announced in the Node Infor-

mation Frame.

- The manufacturer may decide to further enhance the switch by offering a special function, which randomly switches the device on and off. In conjunction with a lamp this function may be used as anti-theft device in the home. At the moment there is no command class defining such a capability. The manufacturer could now ask for approval to implement this function and still be certified as Z-Wave compliant device. Depending on the approval the function would be realized as proprietary function.

# 3.2. Managing Devices

## 3.2.1. Node Information Frame

Each Z-Wave device belongs to a certain device class and is therefore able to support certain command classes. The Node Information Frame is a special message a device can send out to inform other devices about its own capabilities.

The node information frame contains the following information:

- Basic Device Class

- Generic Device Class

- Specific Device Class

- Information if the device is mains powered, battery-operated or FLIRS

- In case it is a FLIRS device, the wakeup frequency (250 ms or 1s)

- A list of all Command Classes the device supports

- Optionally a list of all Command Classes the device is controlling

Figure 3.8 shows the format of the Node Information Frame.
The Node information frame is like a business card of the Z-Wave device. Its used whenever there is a need to announce itself:

- for inclusion into a network.

- for exclusion out of a network.

- when associations are set (for association please refer to chapter 3.3.1).

- when associations are deleted.

- sometime to announce that the device is awake.

Every Z-Wave device must have a way to send out a Node Information Frame. Every device manufacturer has the freedom how to trigger a Node Information Frame be sent. Commonly used implementations are:

- a dedicated button on the outer enclosure of the device or sometimes inside the device.

| 7 | 6 | 5 | 4 | 3 | 2 | 1 | 0 |
|---|---|---|---|---|---|---|---|
| Frame Header | | | | | | | |
| Protocol Information (incl. Basic Device Class) | | | | | | | |
| Generic Device Class | | | | | | | |
| Specific Device Class | | | | | | | |
| Command Class 1 (Support) | | | | | | | |
| ... | | | | | | | |
| Command Class N (Support) | | | | | | | |
| COMMAND_CLASS_MARK | | | | | | | |
| Command Class 1 (Control) | | | | | | | |
| ... | | | | | | | |
| Command Class N (Control) | | | | | | | |

Figure 3.8.: Node Information Frame

- a tamper protection button, typically for PIR and other sensors.

- using the switch paddle of a wall switch.

- using a magnet to switch a magnet sensor inside the device, used when there is no space left or the enclosure if water protected and therefore a button is not suitable.

Because the Node Information Frame is such a universal way to announce the presence of a device the manuals may not explicitly refer to the function. They may refer to a confirmation of inclusion (that means sending out a Node Information Frame) or confirmation of an association (again, on network level this means sending out a Node Information Frame).

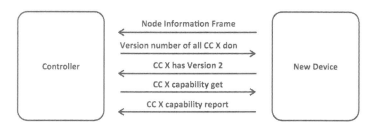

Figure 3.9.: Device Interview Process

## 3.2.2. Interview

During the inclusion process every Z-Wave device sends out its Node Information Frame to the including device, the controller. The controller now knows what kind of device was included. It knows the command classes that are supported and is already able to use the device.

However, certain information is embedded in the command classes and needs to be received by issuing specific commands of these command classes. These commands are referred to as interview commands. The device interview process is demonstrated in Figure 3.9.

### Example 1

The command class meter allows to receive meter values. For this a GET() command is used. The command class however allows to specify what kind of meter values can be reported.

137

If a controller understands that the device is supporting the METER command class, the controller may send the device a command called `SUPPORTEDGET()` to receive a `SUPPORTEDREPORT()`. This report contains a loss of all meter values (W, kWh, m3/h, m3, BTU and others ) the meter is metering.

**Example 2**

The `WAKEUP` command class allows to set the wakeup interval for a battery operated device. It allows to issue a `SET(wakeup interval)` or a `GET()` that causes the device asked to report the actual wakeup interval. The device can however also report a desired wakeup interval. The controller can now decide to just set a certain wakeup interval of choice to the device or to ask the device for its desired value in order to take this into account.

## 3.2.3. Configuration

The Z-Wave standard defines that every device shall be functional on factory defaults right after inclusion. Nevertheless there are devices that may require further user and application specific setups such as

- Sensitivity of a motion detector,

- Behavior of control LED lights,

- Switching delay of an alarm sensor or

- Specific behavior under error conditions.

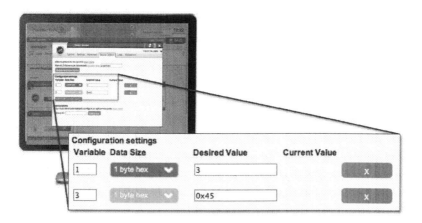

Figure 3.10.: Example of a generic configuration interface in PC Software

The configuration of a device is performed using the optional command class `Configuration`. The configuration command class allows the setting of up to 255 parameters with one value each. A configuration is device specific and all parameters and possible values need to be described in the manufacturers manual.

In order to do a configuration the user needs to know the configuration parameter number and the desired value.

### Example: Configuration of a status LED on a device

Parameter No. 2: switches the LED on the device on, off or blinking according to the status of the device

- Value = 0: Always off

139

- Value = 1: Blinks when active

- Value = 2: Always on

Configurations are typically done using static controllers, either as PC software or an IP gateway. The generic configuration interface according to Figure 3.10 requires the knowledge about the configuration parameter numbers and the meaning of the values to be stored. This information is required to be given in the manual of the device or in the Pepper One database refered to in Annex C.

Modern and more user friendly installation tools maintain a database of known devices with their configuration parameters and possible values. They provide a translation of the values into human-readable explanation and therefore make configuration much easier.

Figure 3.11 shows an example of a user interface with readable explanations of configuration parameters.

## 3.2.4. Battery Management

Battery-operated devices are a special challenge within a Z-Wave network, because they are mostly in a deep sleep state and cannot be reached from a controller in this state.

Battery-operated devices know two states:

- They are awake and can communicate with other devices of the network.

- They are in deep sleep and do not communicate at all. To other controllers they may appear as non existing or damaged.

Figure 3.11.: Example of a user-friendly configuration interface in PC Software

## 3. Z-Wave Application Layer

In order to allow communication with battery-operated devices a mains powered and therefore always active static controller needs to maintain a waiting queue, where all commands are stored which are to be sent to a sleeping device are stored. When the battery-operated device wakes up, it will inform this controller and request the information that is being held for it in mailbox.

At the moment a battery-operated device wakes up it sends a so-called WAKEUP-NOTIFICATION to the controller and stays awake. The WAKEUP-NOTIFICATION indicates to the controller that the battery device is now listening to commands. If all commands are sent, the controller will send a final command NO-MORE-INFO to indicate to the battery device that it can go back to sleeping mode. If the battery-operated device does not receive a NO-MORE-INFO, it will go back to sleeping mode after a defined time. This process of sleeping and wakeup is demonstrated in Figure 3.12.

Most battery-operated devices will have an internal timer, which wakes up the device regularly to check for queued commands. This maximal sleeping time can be configured. A typical sleeping interval is between 30 seconds and several days and can usually be configured on a user interface of the controller. Any change of the wakeup time will, like any other command sent to the battery device, become effective after the next wakeup. Certain devices will limit the wakeup interval to a maximum and minimum value and ignore wakeup intervals that are out of these allowed limits. Figure 3.13 shows an example of a wakeup time dialog.

To allow an initial configuration of a device after inclusion every battery device shall stay awake for a defined time,

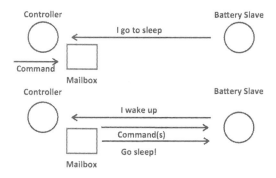

Figure 3.12.: Sleeping and wakeup

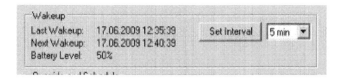

Figure 3.13.: Example of a wakeup time dialog

Figure 3.14.: AAA Battery

which may vary between 20 seconds and some minutes.

Table 3.1 summarized again the different states of a battery operated device and the conditions to change the status.

## 3.2.5. Maximization of battery life time

The battery lifetime is the critical measure of battery-operated devices. Therefore some estimates should be given and taken into account.

- A typical Alkaline-Microcell (AAA) as shown in Figure 3.14 has an energy capacity of approx. 1000 mAh. A typical battery-operated sensor has 2 such batteries.

- A Z-Wave module that uses the very popular Series 300 chip consumes 2.5 $\mu$A in the hibernation state and 21 mA in the wakeup mode. During transmission of packets about 36 mA are required. Table 4.2 shows the current need of the single chip generations in their respective working conditions.

| Situation | Awake | Sleeping |
|---|---|---|
| Inclusion | Right after inclusion | Turns into sleeping mode after a couple of minutes without any further user action. |
| Regularly | Wakes up after a defined interval and sends a notification to static controller. Typical wakeup intervals are between minutes and hours and can be configured by the user within certain boundaries | Controller can turn back the battery-operated device by sending a command. Otherwise the battery device turns back into sleeping mode after a defined time (usually a minute) |
| Local operation of the device | Wakes up on every local operation and communicates status if needed (e.g. button pressed) | Immediately after finishing action |

Table 3.1.: Conditions to change state for battery operated devices

| Chip Generation | Hibernation | Transmitting | Listening |
|---|---|---|---|
| 100 | 31 $\mu$A | 25 mA | 21 mA |
| 200 (since 2005) | 2.5 $\mu$A | 36 mA | 21 mA |
| 300 (since 2007) | 2.5$\mu$A | 36 mA | 21 mA |
| 400 (since 2009) | 1$\mu$A | 23 mA | 21 mA |
| 500 (since 2012) | 1$\mu$A | 23 mA | 15 mA |

Table 3.2.: Power consumptions of different chip generations

- Additional battery power can be used for the devices functionality such as operating an infrared sensor or moving a thermostat valve. This power consumption varies from device to device and is usually minor compared to the power used for the electronics. For the following estimate this portion of the power usage is be neglected.

If a sensor is in the active reception mode, the battery is empty after

$$1000 \text{ mAh} / 21 \text{ mA} = 47 \text{ hours} = 2 \text{ days!}$$

It is therefore mandatory to move a battery-operated device into the deep sleep state for most of the time. The maximum battery lifetime in the deep sleep state is

$$1000 \text{ mAh} / 0.0025 \text{ mA} = 400{,}000 \text{ hours} = 16.666 \text{ days} =$$
$$45 \text{ years.}$$

| Wakeup interval | Battery life time |
|---|---|
| 120 Seconds | 23 days |
| 5 Minutes (typical) | 59 days |
| 30 Minutes | 357 days |
| 24 hours | 46 years |

Table 3.3.: Battery lifetime if no static controller is present

In this time even alkaline batteries will have become empty during this time by self-discharging.

Usually a battery-operated device will wake, send a wakeup notification and wait then for command from the controller including the final command (no more info) to go back in deep sleep. If no commands come back (because the static controller is not reachable or not present or turned down) it is recommended by Z-Wave to keep the device awake for 10 seconds and go back to deep sleep stat automatically. The wakeup interval - this means the amount of times a devices wakes up - will determine the battery life time as shown in Table 3.3.

A battery lifetime of 57 days (ignoring of all local operations like blinking of a LED, moving of a motor etc.!) is still not acceptable. It is therefore very important to keep the static controller in the network to quickly answer all wakeup notifications and shorten the wakeup time of the battery operated devices.

Table 3.4 [1] shows the battery life time for some typical wakeup intervals under the assumption, that the controller

[1]Assumptions are Series 300 chip, 5 ms transmitting time, 50 ms after start sending the device goes back to deep sleep, no further power consumption is taken into account

| Wakeup interval Battery | lifetime |
|---|---|
| 120 Seconds | 4 Years |
| 5 Minutes (typical) | 10 Years |
| 30 Minutes | 29 Years |
| 24 Hours | 45 Years |

Table 3.4.: Battery lifetime with active static controller

is able to send every device back into deep sleep state right after receiving the wakeup - notification.

It is quite obvious that the presence of a static controller significantly extends the battery life time of battery operated devices with wakeup interval. Real battery life time will be substantially shorter since this calculations in Table 3.3 and 3.4 do not take into account

- the application will need to exchange messages (e.g. sending sensor value)

- the controller may not be able to answer the wakeup notification right away minimizing the awake time of the device.

- electronics of the battery operated device will take power as well

- self discharging of the battery

Typical battery life times are between 1 and 2 years for devices with wakeup interval without heavy traffic.

# 3.3. Association versus Scenes

The two previous chapters have explained how devices understand each other in the network and how they can be configured to be used on the network.

While the collecting and displaying of sensor values is a very straightforward process (include the device and access the sensor data in a suitable way) the interrelationship between sensor events, manual interaction and switching of certain devices requires more setup work.

## 3.3.1. Associations

An Association defines a sensor → actor relationship within a network. It is defined as a structure

**IF** (... this and this happens ...) → **THEN** (... do this and that ...)

**Some examples**

> **IF** button 2 is pressed **THEN** ceiling lamp shall go on. **IF** temperature sensor goes above $22°C$, → **THAN** turn down the heating **AND** open the window.

In order to accomplish this kind of IF→ THEN relationship the following requirements need to be met:

- The actor device needs to be identified and able to perform the desired task.

- The sensor or controller needs to be able to generate an event that causes the action.

- The sensor or controller needs to know which actor to control in which way in case the event occurs.

The first requirement is quite obvious. If the ceiling light - to stay in the first example - shall be turned on, the sealing light needs to be controlled by a Z-Wave device that can be turned on and off wirelessly. While this sounds straight forward there are plenty of examples where the actor is not able to fulfill the desired task, e.g. a dimming device cannot change the color of an LED light.

The second requirement is also obvious. There must be a defined event that causes an action. In case a button of a controller is involved, this is quite easy but for sensors that measure constant values this may become a challenge.

Binary sensors such as door sensors or motion detectors generate an event whenever their binary state changed from on (window open) to off (window closed). For a motion detector this already gets more complicated. The motion part - typically resulting in an ON- event is easy to detect but how about the OFF-event.

How can a motion detector be sure that there is no person in the room anymore? Most motion detectors allow to set a certain timeout value and generate an OFF event when the time has run out. It is also imaginable to do nothing after a given time. Even then the motion detector needs to know the minimum time between two events to be generated. Otherwise it will constantly generate events that result in network traffic when a person moves in the room.

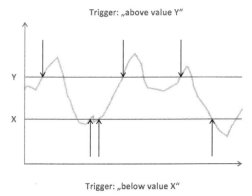

Figure 3.15.: How a trigger works

Timings and settings are typical configuration values of a motion detector and often can be changed either locally using buttons and/or wirelessly using the `Configuration` command class described in chapter 3.2.3.

Sensors that measure an analog value such as temperature, CO2 level, humidity etc. cannot generate an event from just measuring the value. In case the device shall be used to start a IF (...) → THEN (...) association action, they need to know certain boundaries of the measured values and what to do if the measured value reaches the boundary value set. The boundary values that are used to generate events are called trigger values. Figure 3.15 shows how the crossing of a real value and the trigger level creates events.

The third condition is the real core of the association: Devices that are able to perform association means controlling

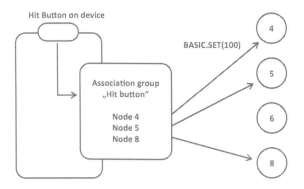

Figure 3.16.: All nodes in association group receive a signal
when the event happens

devices dependent on events offer so called **Association Groups**.

> An Association Group refers to a certain event
> in the device and defines a group of devices that
> will receive a command in case this event hap-
> pens (see Figure 3.16).

This means as an example that every button of a remote control must have at least one association group, because only then it is possible to define devices that shall be operated when the button is pressed.

Association groups are defined by three parameters:

## What is the event?

There are a variety of possible events:

- Pushing a button,

- tampering alarm for a security related product,

- reaching a defined trigger level for a measuring device,

- success or failure of a door lock opening event, etc.

In case of buttons its even possible to have more than one association group:

1. One group may define the devices to be operated at single click of the button.

2. One group may define the devices to be operated at double click of the button.

3. One group may define the devices to be operated when two buttons are pressed.

It can be seen that the number of different association groups is a performance parameter of a given device. It is possible to keep the device simple and cheap by putting different events into one single association group (and let the actor devices find out what to do) or to have different groups for different events.

**How big is the group?**

Due to memory restrictions it is not possible to store all possible 232-1 = 231 devices [2] in an association group. The

---

[2]A Z-Wave network can address 232 devices and an association to the own device does not make sense

number of devices is therefore limited. 5 or 12 devices are a very common number but there are also devices that have association groups with only one single possible actor device.

The number of association groups and the max. number of devices in an association group is very common information to be detected during the device interview described in chapter 3.2.2.

## What command should be sent?

Depending on the kind of actions to be performed the kind of command should be different for each device.

To simplify the setup and management of association groups by far the most devices make the two simplifications:

1. All devices in an association group are controlled by the command class `basic`.

2. All devices in an association group receive the very same command. In case the `Basic` command class is used the value sent with `Basic.Set()` is identical for all devices in one association group.

There is a command class allowing to configure the type of command sent to devices in one association group. The name of the command class is already complicated: `Association Command Configuration` and the implementation is even worse. The result is that only very few devices take advantage of this command class to further specify the type and value of command.

However certain binary sensors at least allow defining what kind of value can be set in case the event happens or the event does not happen anymore.

**Example:**

Default: Door sensor detects open $\rightarrow$ `Basic.Set(1)` is sent
out, Door sensor closes again $\rightarrow$ `Basic.Set(0)` is sent out.
A configuration value allows to turn this relationship to:
open$\rightarrow$ `Basic.Set(0)` and closed $\rightarrow$ `Basic.Set(1)`.

## 3.3.2. Scenes

A scene is a status of a certain part of the home or the whole
home. More precise it is the status of a set of devices in a
home. Therefore scenes are always referred to a situation in
the home. Typical scene descriptions are

- I am coming home

- I am away

- Having Dinner

- Watching TV

The user defines the desired status of different devices at
one moment in a scene:

**Example:**

A scene *'I am away'* would define that the heating is in
energy saving mode, all lights are turned off and the door
is locked.
  If and only if all devices in a scene can be treated similarly
can a scene can be realized with an association group. All
devices in an association group will receive the very same

command if the event happens that was defined as trigger for the association group.

The example above shows that association groups with similar commands to similar devices will not always meet the users requirements. Therefore certain devices offer a more powerful way to handle the situations: **scene activation**.

These devices allow to define a list of devices with a certain well defined command that will be executed when the scene is activated.

### Example: I am away

- `Command Set(0) to Ceiling Light 1`

- `Command Set(0) to Ceiling Light 2`

- `Command Dim(50%) to Outside Lamp`

- `Command Thermostat.Setback() to Central Heating control`

- `Command Lock() to Door Lock Front Door`

- `Command Lock() to Door Lock Back Door`

Similar to association groups there are three requirements to be met:

- The actors need to be identified.

- The controller needs to be able to generate an event.

- The controller needs to know which actor to control in which way.

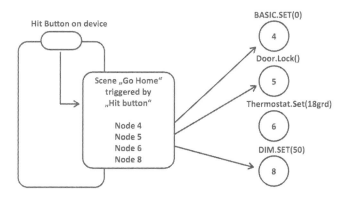

Figure 3.17.: Scene execution

Compared to associations the setup of a scene is more complicated because there are individual commands to be defined for each device that participates in the scene. Furthermore there are many more data to be stored in a controller than for a simple association. This is the reason that only few devices support scenes compared to almost all sensors and controllers that support association groups. Figure 3.17 shows a scene execution.

Scenes are typically found in three different types of devices.

- Certain remote controls offer few extra scenes beside plenty of association groups. Typically they have dedicated buttons for scenes beside the standard control buttons for individual devices or groups of devices. The Universal Remote Control from Merten (Euro-

3. Z-Wave Application Layer

pean Device) or the Z-Wave Remote Control from ACT (US-Device) are examples.

- There are dedicated scene controllers that are typically wall mountable or designed for desktops and capable of storing multiple scenes and execute them. Examples here are the scene wall controllers from Leviton or Cooper (both US devices).

- The by far most popular way to define scenes are IP Gateways. The biggest advantage of IP gateways is the large user interface like a web browser that makes the setup of scenes much easier. Beside this there is plenty of memory to store all scene relevant data.

Normal buttons for association groups control have an ON and an OFF function to turn on or off the devices associated. Long press is typically used to execute dimming functions for dimmer connected. Scene controllers don't have an ON or OFF. The reason is that its not trivial to deactivate a scene. This would mean that all devices need to go back to the status they had before the scene is activated. The scene controller would have to check the status of all devices and store their value before executing the commands defined for the given scene activation. This would take too much time and effort so that so far no scene controller manufacturer is following this path. Another option is to turn all devices back into a predefined status e.g. `all off`. This however can also be seen as a scene (a set of devices is turned into well defined status) and it is handled exactly in this way.

Therefore scene controllers only activate a scene but don't deactivate them anymore. Scene controllers that offer a de-

Figure 3.18.: In-Wall Scene Controller, manufactured by Cooper

activation button for a scene typically just turn off all devices connected to the very scene. Figure 3.18 shows the cooper scene controller as an example. Pushing a scene activation button executes the scene defined for this button and a blue LED turns on to indicate that this scene was executed last. Its possible to "turn off" the scene but only by executing another scene or by hitting the same button again. In this case all devices operated in the scene are turned off. Users need to make sure that only devices, that can handle the OFF command (`basic.Set(0)`) properly are operated by this scene.

**How to setup scenes in a scene controller**

Most scene controllers allow to setup scenes wirelessly via Z-Wave using software. If no software is available for configuration some remote controls offer a nice tool: Scene Snapshot.

1. The first step is to assign all devices that shall be operated by a given scene to a single scene control button.

2. All these devices are now turned to the desired status. Certain light may go on, some may go off and dimmer may go to a certain dimming state.

3. A special command e.g. a long press of the scene button activates a process where the scene controller asks all devices for the status and stores this very status as scene.

Any press of the given scene activation button will now restore the same situation that was created and stored before.

Figure 3.19.: Scene setting in Z-Way Z-Wave Gateway

This is a very convenient way to setup a scene if there is no large screen interface for management.

**How to setup scenes in an IP gateway**

Most scenes will be defined and stored in IP Gateways. Figure 3.19 shows an example of a user interface to define scenes. Devices can be added and device status information can be given. Most powerful gateways may even offer the possibility to write scripts in a given language to implement complicated setups and scenes. They will then allows to delay certain execution of commands or make the execution of a command dependent on certain devices status or even information provided by internet services.

An example network has the following functions:

- An external rain sensor that offers a status information that is either 1 (it is raining) or 0 (it is not raining).

- A window motor to turn **on** or **off** the roof window.

- A jalousie controller that is opening or closing the window blind.

A script for this function may look like:

Listing 3.1: Pseudo Script Code to control a window

```
 7  if rainsensor.status != 1:
 8          windowMotorControl.Set(0) // close the window
 9          while windowMotorControl.status != 0:
10              sleep 1;
11          jalousieController.Set(100)
12  else:
13  jalousieController.Set(0)
14          while jalousieController.status != 0:
15              sleep 1;
16          windowMotorControl.Set(100) // close the window
```

The first and very obvious function is that the window is closed when it is raining and that the window is open when it is not raining. The window however should not be opened if the blind is closed because for some mechanical reasons the opening blind will destroy the blind. The script is therefore waiting for the jalousie to close until the status of the motor control indicates that the window is closed(status=0). In case it is not raining the jalousie will open first and only when the `jalousieController.status` indicated that the jalousie is really open, the command for opening the window is issued.

Figure 3.20.: Example of a User Interface defining timers and schedules

Scripts in gateways allow defining and realizing very complex relationships and dependencies.

In-wall scene controllers or in remote control scenes are always activated by pushing a button. IP gateway with their computing power and their big and nice user interfaces offer more options that finally allow to implement heavily automated and complex controls in the home.

1. Execution by time: IP Gateways usually have an internal clock that can be used to create scene activation events. These events can be

   - single time: on July 7th, 2012, 8:45

   - periodical per day: every Friday morning 09:00

163

Figure 3.21.: Example of a User Interface defining Boolean rules and logic

- frequently: every minute

Figure 3.20 shows the example of an user interface that allows to define timers.

2. Execution by pushing a manual button on a remote control or a scene controller

3. Execution activated by sensor value: the *I am home* scene gets activated when the Motion detector detects a person entering the house.

4. A combination of times, manual button presses and events from sensors. Figure 3.21 shows an example of such combination. Boolean logic or AND and OR is applied to combine different events.

Figure 3.22 shows the automation architecture of Z-Way, a Z-Wave control software and gateway[Z-Way2012]. It shows the interrelationship of Timer settings, Scene activation, the combination (rules) engine, the events generated by Z-Wave devices and the resulting commands to Z-Wave devices.

### 3.3.3. Scene Activation

The definition and activation of scenes is based on a set of special command classes for scene handling.

- `Scene activation` that's the event that activates the scenes. It contains a scene ID to specify what scene to activate.

- `Scene controller configuration` is used to assign association groups to scene IDs. As a result a triggered

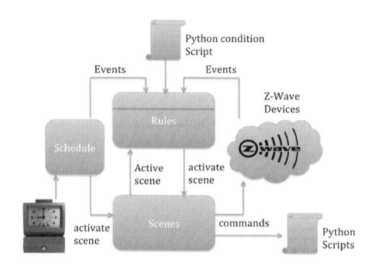

Figure 3.22.: Automation Architecture of Z-Way, a Z-Wave
software and gateway

association group will send out a certain scene activation ID instead of normal control commands sent out from association groups. This command class is a sub function of Association Command Configuration Command Class.

- `Scene Actuator Configuration` - It is possible to predefine how certain actuators will handle a scene activation command. This command class results from the idea to define the scene in the actors and just send out a scene activation command that turns actuators accordingly. Only very few devices support this function and there it is not used anymore.

This limits the scene handling to devices that explicitly support scene activation.

### Approaches in IP Gateways to receive Scene Information

Users however want to use all kind of devices to activate scenes, particularly wall controllers, remote controls and even sensors. Most of them were never designed for scene activation and therefore only support associations or sometimes not even this.

This creates the challenge in that the IP gateways

- receive messages from the devices that were not designed for scene activation.

- They need to interpret them as scene commands.

- They need to distinguish different events from the same device in order to activate different scenes.

167

To accomplish this, IP gateways use certain approaches to enable scene activation even for devices that were not initially designed for scene activation .

## Scene Activation

As described above certain Z-Wave controllers already explicitly support the activation of scenes. Their different buttons can be configured to send enumerated scene activation commands, which are received by the controller. Controllers with scene switching capability can be used for scene switching without further work and constrains by IP gateways.

## Associations

Associations, sometimes referred to as Links, are used to establish switching relationship between a controlling and a controlled Z-Wave device. Typically controlling devices send a BASIC SET command to perform a switching function in the controlled device.

If these BASIC switching commands are sent from a controller to central intelligent 'master' controller they can be interpreted as a scene switching command. The big challenge is that the BASIC SET command does not allow sending any scene number information. Rather the BASIC SET command typically only supports the values 0x00 and 0xff. As long as the sending controller only has one push button or just one association group supported, a received BASIC SET command can be used to trigger to a scene easily.

If the sending controller device has more than one association group, the intelligent 'master' controller is not able to differentiate between the different groups as they all send the very same BASIC SET command. The result is that certain buttons do not issue any command or all buttons will issue the very same command.

## Multi Channel Association

If the sending controller can send multi channel commands it can be configured in a way to send different scene activation commands (still as BASIC SET or BASIC REPORT with values 0x00 or 0xff) to different channels helping the intelligent 'master' controller to distinguish different commands and activate different scenes accordingly. In order to use this "trick" the sending controller must support multi channel association.

## Virtual Nodes

In some cases the intelligent 'master' controller is able to act as multiple virtual nodes in the network. It will then not only receive commands for one single Node ID but for multiple Node IDs. Associations can be set for each of these different Node IDs that are all received by the same physical device. The intelligent 'master' controller is now able to distinguish different commands and activate different scenes accordingly. In order to use this trick the hardware used for the intelligent 'master' controller (USB Stick, Set Top Box, IP Gateway) must support bridged devices. Only few devices do this at the moment.

| Points of discussion | Association Groups | Scenes |
|---|---|---|
| Easiness of setup | Very easy | More complicated |
| Switching by remote controls and wall controllers | Easy | May be complicated |
| Works, when IP gateway or Cloud Service is down | Yes | No |
| Activated by timers | Not possible | Possible |
| Mix of different switching status | Not possible | Possible |
| Activated by web interface | Not possible | Possible |

Table 3.5.: Comparison of scenes and associations

## 3.3.4. Comparison of Association Groups and Scenes

Both associations and scenes are suitable to control relationships between sensors, controllers and actors. They can be even mixed. However it is recommended to stay with one concept to make the setup of the network easier.

Table 3.5 shows a comparison of scenes and associations with their pros and cons:

The net-net of this comparison is that associations are easier to use but limited in their functionality. Scenes may be more complicated but give users much more flexibility and power to define interdependencies and automation of the Z-Wave network.

# 3.4. User Interfaces

The user interface is the final building block to form a smart home control solution based on Z-Wave. There is no right or wrong way to create a user interface. User interfaces depend on style, local preferences, type, knowledge and skills of the people using it (... and yes, also the people creating it). It is also far beyond the scope of this book to describe the details of all user interfaces on the market in details. The Z-Wave standard defines very few aspects of the user interface leaving plenty of room for creativity on the manufacturers side.

However, some general guidelines seem to be similar across the different products and manufacturers choices:

## 3.4.1. Wall controllers and remote controls

Wall controllers and remote controls only have buttons to interact with and LEDs or very small LCD panels to indicate status.

In case there is a LCD panel, setup, management and control is quite easy. In case there are only LEDs with one or with different colors, study of the device manual is usually required to decrypt the codes shown. A lot of wall controller or remote control maker use

- red LEDs to indicate errors,

- green LEDs to indicate success,

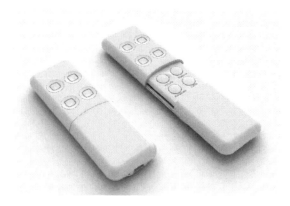

Figure 3.23.: Dedicated buttons on a Z-Wave remote control

- flashing LEDs to indicate the transmission of data,

- slow blinking LEDs to indicate that the device is in a certain state, e.g. ready for inclusion.

Figure 3.23 shows a remote control that has dedicated buttons for Inclusion, Exclusion, Learn Mode and Association below a slideable cover plus 4 control buttons for scene control.

## 3.4.2. Installer tools

Installer tools are special software tools that are used only during the installation and setup of the network. They typically don't provide a user interface for daily usage but very detailed technical data for professionals.

Four functions are mainly covered by installer tools.

1. Inclusion, Exclusion

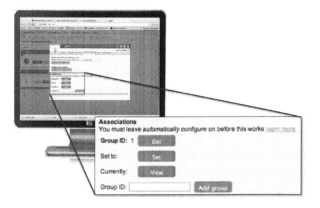

Figure 3.24.: Simple and generic Association setup interface
- VERA IP Gateway

2. Setting of Configuration Parameters as described in chapter 3.2.3

3. Management of Associations

4. Management of Routing

Associations can be set using very generic interfaces as seen in Figure 3.24. More user friendly interfaces either use drag'n drop (as shown in Figure 3.25) or drawing lines to visualize the relationship between sender and receiver. Figure 3.26, the MERTEN CONNECT installer tool, is shown as an example of such a user interface.

## 3.4.3. Web-Interfaces for Users

Interfaces for users focus on three basic functions:

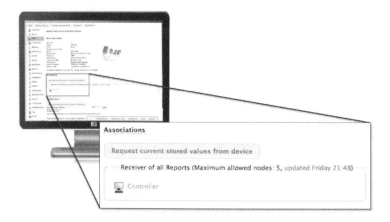

Figure 3.25.: Drag'n Drop setup for Association relationships - Z-Way Software

1. Visualization of Sensor Values

2. Direct control of actors

3. Activation of Scenes

Depending on the technology used and the display screen real estate these user interfaces can be quite simple or heavily animated. Quite often the devices in the Z-Wavenetwork can be placed on a floor plan or at least assigned to a certain room.

Figure 3.27 shows an example of a very basic WEB UI for smart phones that can be shown on typical hardware such as iPhone, Android Phone or Blackberry. Other Interfaces may be more stylish but rarely provide substantially more functionality.

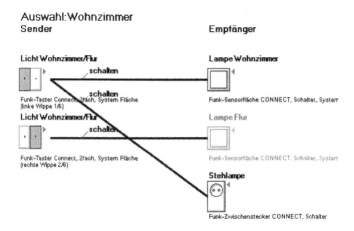

Figure 3.26.: Drawing lines to visualize associations -
Merten CONNECT Installer tool

Figure 3.27.: Example of a smart home user interface on a
mobile device

# 4. Z-Wave in action - Tips and Tricks

This chapter will provide some useful and practical tips how to build, manage and use a Z-Wave network.

## 4.1. Building the network - general workflow

Every Z-Wave network is built following the same steps:

1. define the desired functions

2. pick the right devices

3. include all devices into one network

4. configure the devices according to the users need

5. set all association and define all scenes

6. do some final housekeeping work

## 4.1.1. Defining the desired functions

A smart home can have plenty of functions and the planning process can be overwhelming. It makes sense to clearly define the high level services first. These services should be broken down by rooms or floors and by the basic functions of an intelligent home network:

- light,

- heating,

- climate,

- security,

- safety,

- door lock,

- media and entertainment,

- energy management,

- windows.

This is a high level list with items that may overlap with each other. Having as example a window open-close control this is both - a security feature and a climate control feature.

A second step is to define where the smart home shall be controlled from:

- Wall controllers - where placed?

- Remote controls - how many?

- Smart Phone

- Web Browser

- Wall panel

The third step of planning is to create a list of all rooms or floors and assign what functions shall be available in what rooms. There may be functions that are applied to all rooms and functions that only apply to the whole home as such. Such a list might look like this

- Sleeping room: safety (smoke), light, window control

- Kitchen: light, heating, safety(smoke + water leakage), window control

- Living room: light, heating, media

- All rooms: energy management

- House: main door control, back door control

A few advantages of Z-Wave are that it

- can be used to retrofit existing homes and

- can be applied step by step overtime.

**If the planning of a whole home looks too big or expensive or complicated, it is no problem to start with a very small network focusing on one or two applications.** Typical small and single focus networks may solve problems like:

- Only managing the main door to avoid phone calls like "I forgot my key"

- Just combining a second wall switch beside the bed to avoid the typical way to get into the bedroom: turn on ceiling light → work to bed → turn on bed light → work back to door → turn off sealing light → work back to bed → go to bed → turn off bed light

- Installing a central energy meter to get an idea when the most energy is consumed.

- Being able to turn off all big standby consumers such as computers, TV, HIFI etc. when leaving the home.

- Being able to turn up the heat while being on the way home.

These solutions can easily be expanded step by step. This is one of the big advantages of wireless technologies in general and Z-Wave in particular

## 4.1.2. Picking the right devices

The selection of the devices is a complex task, because multiple aspects need to be taken into consideration:

- Light control:
  - What kind (color, shape) of wall control elements are suitable?
  - Shall light be switched or dimmed?
  - What kind of lighting elements are installed (traditional light, high voltage halogen, low voltage halogen, LED, CFL)?

  - What kind of power wiring system is available in the house (2 wire or 3 wire cabling)?

  - How many lights are there per room? Are they wired - like ceiling or wall lamps or do they stand alone - like a floor light?

- Heating:

  - What kind of heating system is already installed or planned and how is it to be controlled (central boiler, floor heating with central control, floor heating with zones, radio thermostats, 240 V controlled HVAC,...)?

  - Shall the heating be controlled in the room with local elements?

  - Is heating and cooling combined?

- Doors:

  - What kind of doors are used (thickness, locking system, dimension of door)?

  - Shall there be handles on the outside, are the doors left/right winged?

  - Which colors and finishes will match do the doors best?

- Windows:

  - Shall the windows just be monitored or also moved?

  - Roof windows or standard windows?

  - What kind of jalousie controller shall be installed ?

- Energy Management:

> – What devices beyond lighting and heating shall me
> monitored (Dish Washer, washing machine, freezer,
> fridge, sauna, computer)?

This book does not intend to give correct product recommendations but to list down the right questions. There are well organized online shops and home automation professional available for help in picking the devices and calculating the costs. Two links to major sites can be found in the Annex C.

---

Here are some more technical Z-Wave related constrains for device picking:

- If there is at least one battery-operated sensor or actor (FLIRS devices are ok), there must be a static controller like an IP gateway.

- If devices shall be controlled from a web browser or a smart phone, an IP gateway is a must too.

- Battery-operated devices cannot route. If a network only consists of battery-operated devices, there is no routing and the wireless coverage is limited. Its recommended to have a fair distribution of mains powered devices to maintain network functions and network stability.

---

## 4.1.3. Including everything into a single network

Unless there are very special requirements or super large networks all devices shall be included into one single wireless network. A Z-Wave network can manage up to 232 devices, however a typical amount of nodes in a fully equipped home is in the range of 50 to 80. This means there is plenty of room for future expansion and enhancements.

A Z-Wave network is built by a controller. There is always one single primary controller that is responsible for the network. In case there is an IP gateway available this IP gateway should be picked as main controller simply because the user interface is very convenient and the IP gateway offers backup and restore functions in case something goes wrong.

If no IP gateway is available, any other controller can act as primary controller and the role of the primary controller can also be handed over to a different controller when desired.

For the setup and the configuration of a network it may even be desirable to have different controllers to do the work. All inclusions can be done with a remote control as primary controller and the role of the primary controller is then handed over to an IP gateway for further operations. The IP gateway may however have to reconfigure all devices to make sure the wakeup interval targets are set correctly and all information generated during the device interview are available.

It's also possible to do it the other way around. An IP gateway of software may be very beneficial for the setup work even if the network is later only operated by wall controllers and remote controls. The software then acts as an installer tool just for setup and configuration.

## Bring the prophet to the mountain or the mountain to the prophet?

Chapter 2.10.3 already explained the difference between the two main ways to organize networks: Explorer Frames and SUC/SIS. If

- the device to be included does not support Explorer Frame or

- the controller itself does not support Explorer Frame or

- there is no sufficient amount of Explorer Frame capable devices in the network to ensure routing of Explorer Frames,

the network will not benefit from the Explorer Frame and new devices MUST be in direct radio range to the including controller.

There are two options for this:

1. Bringing all devices to the controller, include them and then install them in the final location.

2. Installing all devices at their final location and use a mobile controller for inclusion into the network.

Option (1) means to always change the network right after a device was included because the device moves to a different location within the network. This requires a network rediscovery be performed right after the device was installed at its final location. The network rediscovery process will certainly manage all mains powered devices and update all routing tables accordingly but may fail for battery-operated devices for reasons mentioned in chapter 2.10.3. Additionally all devices that will be mains operated and powered by fixed wires in the wall need to be powered temporarily just for inclusion when brought to the controller location.

Option (2) requires a mobile controller. Even then the management of battery-operated devices remains an issue. The popular IP Gateway VERA from Micasaverde follows this approach.

**What happens if I don't care at all about all this SUC and Explorer Frame stuff?** Well, in 99% of the cases nothing will happen and the network will just work fine. However, according to Murphy's Law it's the 1 % that will kick in at the wrong moment and the wrong place. So it's recommended to understand what is going on behind the scene to know what to do given a mixed set of devices and a network problem.

## 4.1.4. General Inclusion Guidelines

The basic process of inclusion of a device is described in chapter 2.6.3.

- The controller must be in the inclusion mode.

- The device to be included must not be included already, factory fresh or reset.

- The device to be included must be in direct range of the controller unless the network supports Explorer Frames.

- The device needs to issue a Node Information Frame that will trigger the controller to configure the device and include it into the network.

Wall controllers or remote controls typically have either dedicated buttons for inclusion like shown in Figure 4.1 -or they use a special key sequence to turn the controller into the inclusion mode.

The inclusion mode is indicated by a blinking LED or by any other reasonable way. The inclusion mode typically times out if no inclusion takes place. If the controller was successfully including a device, it will either terminate the inclusion mode or continue with the inclusion until the mode times out or a special button terminates the inclusion mode. The behavior depends on the manufacturers implementation. Please refer to the manual of the controller for further details.

IP gateways or Z-Wave control software solutions follow the same process. They offer virtual buttons for inclusion and for exclusion and will indicate when the inclusion mode is active and when it was terminated. Figure 4.2 shows an example of a user interface of a Z-Wave software indicating that it is in active inclusion mode.

The device to be included needs to issue a Node Information Frame signifying that it wants to be included. That's why there is always at least one button that can be used to send the Node Information Frame. Different solutions can be found in the market:

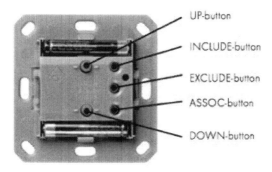

Figure 4.1.: Wall Controller with special button for inclusion

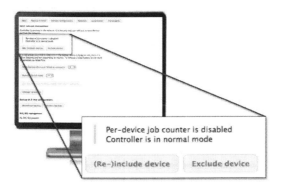

Figure 4.2.: Example of Inclusion Function in PC software

**INCLUSION OF ADDITIONAL DEVICES:**

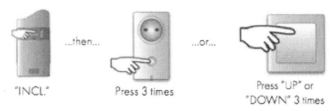

Figure 4.3.: Example of a manual describing of the inclusion process

- Single click of the button;

- Triple click of the button within a certain time- time may vary;

- Hold the button for a defined time and release it then.

Please refer to the manual of the device on how to be included into a Z-Wave Network. Figure 4.3 shows an example of a manual with the description of the inclusion process.

There are a couple of reasons why an inclusion can fail. **The by far most important reason is that the device to be included was already included in a different network.** The simple fix of this problem is to use the exclusion function of the controller to exclude the device first before it gets included again. Exclusion can be done by any controller not only the controller that was used for inclusion.

## 4.1.5. Inclusion of controllers

The inclusion of a controller by another controller works similar to the inclusion of any other device. Behind the scenes the primary controller will transmit all network data to the new controller that is now a secondary controller.

> If the device to be included is a controller, this devices cannot be included by pressing an inclusion button! Pressing the inclusion button will turn the device into inclusion mode and then it will try to include other devices. To be included into a different network a controller needs to be turned into the so called LEARN-Mode. Like the Inclusion Mode the learn mode will also be indicated by a LED sequence or a special message on software and it will also be timed out if no inclusion happens.
>
> Refer to the manual on information how to include a controller as secondary controller into a network or how to turn the controller into Learn-Mode.

Figure 4.4 shows the process of including a controller as secondary controller. It is also possible to include a new controller into the network and hand over the primary controller function to this new controller. The process is the same but the primary controller needs to be turned into a special mode called Primary Change, Primary Shift or Controller Shift. The other controller needs to be in the learn mode as well and both modes will time out similar to the normal inclusion mode.

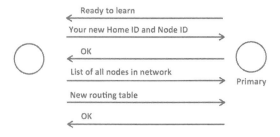

Figure 4.4.: Controller-Replication

Please refer to the manual of the controller if and how this controller supports the primary change functions. Not all controllers support this function. Figure 4.5 shows the user interface of software supporting this function.

## 4.1.6. Inclusion of battery-operated devices

The big challenge of battery-operated devices is the deep sleep state. Once the battery is included the device should go right into deep sleep state but wake up when a button is pressed.

However, there are bad implementations of battery-operated devices that may cause trouble:

- They do not go into deep sleep right after batteries are inserted because they wait for an inclusion. If they get never included they will waste valuable battery lifetime.

- If nothing happens, they will go into deep sleep and

Figure 4.5.: Example of Primary Change Function in PC software

not wake up anymore. It's impossible then to include the device.

The certification process meanwhile ensures that all new devices behave properly, but in order to avoid confusion it's recommended to follow these guidelines:

1. Include every battery-operated device right after inserting the batteries. Make sure to configure a reasonable wake-up time before the device goes into deep sleep state for the first time.

2. In case there is further configuration work needed set a low wake-up interval first but make sure that you configure a longer battery saving wakeup interval when all configuration work is finished. Alternatively its possible to wakeup the device manually for finishing the configuration work.

3. Do not include and configure multiple devices at once and don't lose any time after inserting batteries and initial inclusion.

4. A reasonable wake-up time is a trade-off between two goals:

   - A very long wake-up interval will save battery capacity but may create problems in case of network rediscovery. The static controller may not receive anything from the battery device during the rediscovery and then assume the device as not functioning.

   - A very short wakeup time helps the controller to keep track of the device but costs battery lifetime.

5. The wake-up interval must be configured between the allowed boundaries. Refer to the manual of the manufacturer for more information about reasonable wakeup times. Reasonable wake-up intervals are between 15 minutes and a couple of days depending on the function of the device.

## 4.1.7. Configuration

The second step after inclusion is the configuration of the devices. For the reason and the general approach of configuration please refer to chapter 3.2.3. Changing configuration values in software or IP in gateways can be very efficient depending on the device type:

- **Mains powered devices:** right after saving or confirming the configuration parameter change in the user interface of the configuration tool

- **FLIRS devices:** right after saving or confirming the configuration parameter change in the user interface of the configuration tool

- **Battery-operated devices with periodical wake-up:** After the new configuration parameters are saved in the software the devices need to wake up. This may take as long as the defined wake-up interval. Attention: If the wake-up interval was changed, the device is still in deep sleep for the time period of the previous setting. Only after successfully sending the new wake-up interval setting to the device the device will change its wakeup behavior. It is possible and recommended to manually wake up the device to speed up the process. Please refer to the manual of the device how to manually wake up the device.

- **Battery-powered portable controller:** After the new configuration parameters are saved in the software the devices need to be manually woken up in order to allow the controller to store the new configuration values in the device.

Certain devices will not wakeup if wakeup is not configured correctly. If they don't know where to send the wakeup notification to they will simply stay quite. Other devices solve the situation by sending a wakeup notification as broadcast command. As long as the primary controller is within wireless of the device waking up this will work fine.

## 4.1.8. Association and Scenes

It's possible to mix scenes and associations but it is recommended to stay with one system just for simplification.

Associations make much sense when there are simple and direct control relationships such as motion detector → light. It would only make the whole system more complicated to have this relation done using a gateway scene. Additionally, the direct control relationship between the motion detector and the light is more reliable - simply because there is less communication involved.

As soon as there are more complex switching setups needed scenes in gateways are the better choice.

Similar to configuration settings also association settings need to be stored in the device before they become effective. For the different behavior on when this will happen after storing the association in the installer tool or IP gateway please refer to chapter 4.1.7.

# 4.2. Housekeeping - How to get a stable network?

Z-Wave is a quite robust wireless network that will work out of the box. Nevertheless there are some housekeeping rules and guidelines to be taken into account. They are intended to make the network more stable and more robust.

## 4.2.1. Radio Layer

Here are some tips to avoid problems on the radio layer:

- Avoid metal wall boxes whenever possible. It is possible to run Z-Wave within a metal box but it may attenuate the radio signal. There are vendors that have designed products particularly for application in metal boxes and the mje majority of products may have problems in such an environment.

- Check the minimum wireless range and follow the recommendation given in section 2.3 in regard to radio shadow, installation height, reflection etc. **Try to position all devices with a minimum distance of 30 cm from large metal constructions.**

- The fact that a Z-Wave network works properly during installation is no guarantee that it will work 24 by 7. There are plenty of ways to change the radio signal situation in a home. Even small changes like moving furniture or opening/closing a door may have impact. This is rare but not impossible.

Certain installer tools or software solutions visualize the routing table of a network. They show whether or not two nodes have a direct radio link. Certain tools also measure the round trip time of radio signals to estimate the quality of a radio link.

This is a section of the Z-Way users manual explaining the function [Z-Way2012]:

**Communication Timing Statistics  Expert Mode only**

*In expert mode the bottom context menu offers Communication Timing Stats. This opens an*

**Communication timing statistics**                                                    ✕

| Node | Type | Total | OK | SOSO | FAIL | last packets (in 10 ms units) |
|------|------|-------|-----|------|------|-------------------------------|
| Node 2 | mains | 1144 pkts | 99% | 0% | 0% | 1 1 1 1 1 1 1 1 1 1 1 1 1 1 1 |
| Node 3 | flirs 1000 | 3429 pkts | 99% | 0% | 0% | 116 233 116 116 118 116 116 116 116 115 115 115 116 |
| Node 4 | battery | 11 pkts | 90% | 0% | 9% | 1 4 1 1 1 1 1 1 1 1 4 1 |
| Node 5 | mains | 1144 pkts | 99% | 0% | 0% | 1 1 1 1 1 5 3 5 13 5 1 1 1 1 1 |
| Node 7 | mains | 381 pkts | 99% | 0% | 0% | 2 2 1 1 1 1 1 1 1 1 1 1 1 1 |
| Node 8 | mains | 380 pkts | 99% | 0% | 0% | 1 1 3 1 1 1 1 1 1 1 1 1 1 1 |
| Node 9 | mains | 1142 pkts | 99% | 0% | 0% | 1 2 1 6 4 1 6 4 1 1 1 1 1 1 1 |
| Node 11 | battery | 139 pkts | 95% | 0% | 3% | 1 4 1 1 1 1 8 1 1 7 1 1 1 1 1 |
| Node 12 | mains | 381 pkts | 99% | 0% | 0% | 1 1 7 1 1 1 1 1 1 1 2 1 1 1 1 |
| Node 13 | battery | 63 pkts | 100% | 0% | 0% | 1 1 1 1 1 1 1 1 1 1 1 1 5 1 1 |
| Node 14 | mains | 1786 pkts | 53% | 0% | 45% | 5 4 1 4 9 3 9 1 11 2 9 9 1 1 1 |

Figure 4.6.: Z-Way vizualises the message traveling times

*extra window to show some communication timing statistics that are very useful to find communication problems.*

*Z-Way measures the time between sending a command from the controller to a certain node and receiving a final acknowledgement from this node. These timings are shown on the right hand side for the different nodes. The minimum time between sending and receiving a confirmation is 10 ms (equals 1 in the table). If the packet needs to be resent, this time may increase. As long as the time value is still marked green there was only a collision in the air or any other need for retransmission. A black entry indicates that the controller was not able to reach the given node with three attempts and tried a different route that finally worked. A red entry indicates that the communication finally failed after some re-routing attempts.*

*For FLIRS devices (Frequently listening battery nodes) the minimum timing is about 1 second since a wake-up beam need to wake up the device first. Hence the timings for these nodes are generally longer.*

*The example of a real network shown above allows the following conclusions:*

- *Most nodes communicate most of the time without any problems.*

- *The FLIRS Node 2 shows a longer communication time but due to the nature of FLIRS this is acceptable.*

- *Node 4 and Node 11 had one failed communication. For battery-powered devices it sometimes happens that the final go back to sleep command is sent out too late and the device is already back in sleep mode. In this case the particular communication may fail which is not necessarily an indication for a network problem.*

- *Node 14 shows failed communication and a lot of frames that were only successfully transmitted after several attempts. Since no other routes succeeded it can be concluded that the device is just at the edge of the wireless range of the controller and using other routes do not offer any advantage.*

> *Here it would be recommended to place an-*
> *other node between Node 14 and any other*
> *node which may act as router in this case.*
> *The fact that sometimes the controller can*
> *reach Node 14 (indicated by 1) directly with-*
> *out routing suggests, that one additional de-*
> *vice between the controller and Node 14 will*
> *certainly improve the communication.*

## 4.2.2. Z-Wave Networking and Routing

To get a stable network that works well according to user
expectation there are some general goals to be met:

- Avoid any traffic to nodes that will not respond anymore.

- Avoid any unneeded traffic to keep the air free for the
  real important messages.

- Make sure all devices always know to communicate to
  each other.

This translates into the following practical recommendations:

1. Exclude not longer needed devices or outside thats are
   moved outside the network. If one device it taken from
   the network - e.g. a wall plug by just unplugging - the
   device should be excluded from the network. Otherwise this device is not reached anymore and will create
   overhead traffic until it's marked as failed.

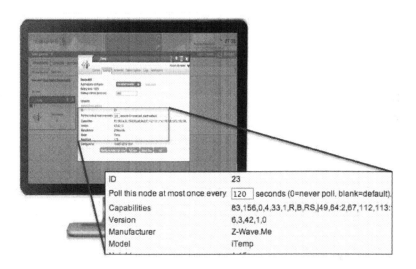

Figure 4.7.: User Interface to allow individual polling

2. If a device is obviously failed or broken, remove it from the controller. Controllers typically have functions to remove failed nodes.

3. Don't forget to remove all disappeared nodes from all association groups where they were included once. The device having this association group will otherwise always try to communicate with these lost devices creating delay and waste valuable battery life time.

4. If a device is moved within the network, a network reorganization is always needed.

5. Try to avoid longer routes since they increase the chance of routing failures. Z-Wave allows routes up to 4 hops (refer to chapter 2.7 for details) however longer routes with more than 2 intermediate nodes tend to be unstable.

6. The worst case scenario for thr routing algorithm is a device that is just in wireless range but drops out of direct range from time to time. Whenever the device is in direct range direct range communication wil be used any all routed as discontinued. Whenever direct range does not work anymore the alorithms will need to redetect a valid route again causing a lof of traffic in the network. The communciation timing function shown in Figure 4.6 is an excellent tool to find these links.

7. Reduce Polling intensity. Every controller will poll all nodes from time to time to see if they are alive or to call certain status values. Its desired to poll very

often to always have very updated values available in
the controller. Heavy polling however creates a lot of
traffic in the network and should therefore be limited.
Some controllers only allow to set polling intervals for
the whiole network while others even allow to define
polling behavior for every device. Figure 4.7 shows a
user interface of the IP Gateway VERA that allows to
set polling intervals for every device.

a) Choose the poll time that is reasonable. It's not
   recommended to pull more often than once per
   minute, even 5 minutes is a very reasonable number.

b) Don't poll FLIRS devices.

c) Try to enable unsolicited reporting of sensor values wherever possible. Most metering devices
   (power, temperature) allow to be configured so
   that they send sensor updates frequently or when
   changes occur. Make heavy use of these functions
   and limit the polling of the corresponding command classes.

d) Sensors report the value of the actual moment
   while meters accumulate values. meters should
   therefore nore be polled more often than once
   per hour or even less.

e) If there is already one devices class polled deliv-
   ering the status of a device e.g. switch binary
   command classes for a binary switch, there is no
   need to poll additional command classes- e.g. the
   basic command class- to get the very same value.

Network reorganization is also a good prevention method and it is recommended after any change of the network (include device, exclude devices remove failed nodes, move nodes). Please be aware that changes in the environment such as new furniture may also change the wireless communication environment. A regular network reorganisation is therefore a good practice to keep the network healthy and stable.

The net-net of these recommendations are:

- Avoid metal surfaces closer than 30 cm.

- use Explorer Frame capable device as much as you can

- avoid wireless links that are at the corner of direct range

- get rid of all deivces not used anymore.

- perform a network reorganization afetr ever change of the network

## 4.3. Known Problems and Trouble Shooting

In general Z-Wave is a very stable and easy to use technology. However, it needs to be taken into account that users have to deal with technologies of different manufacturers, different quality of documentation and different quality of products.

**Z-Wave guarantees interoperability but not quality**.

With over 700 different products introduced over the course of 10 years there are certain differences in functionality of devices. Here is a list of typical challenges, pitfalls and problems:

## 4.3.1. Mismatch of Language

The Z-Wave alliance enforces the use for common language for the most criticial processes and functions of Z-Wave:

- Inclusion and Exclusion

- Association

- Meshing and Routing

Every term beyond this short list may be interpreted differently by different manufacturers. Manuals in other languages than English bear another reason for confusion, since local language translations even of the core terms of Z-Wave are not monitored and controlled by the Z-Wave Alliance.

## 4.3.2. Mismatch of functions

In order to simplify the use of Z-Wave some manufacturers have combined the steps inclusion and association into one step. Particularly remote controls may just allow to *include a new device to a group*. This is a description of an association. Knowledable Z-Wave users will miss the first step always needed - the inclusion. The remote control combines both functions into one. This is not necessarily a bad idea but it may create confusion.

Figure 4.8.: 1st generation Z-Wave product, made by Advanced Control Technologies

### 4.3.3. No forward compatibility

The core value of Z-Wave is interoperability. This is maintained among others by making sure that all new devices are backward compatible to existing products. As a result it is still possible to use a first generation product that is 10 years old in todays modern networks. Taking into account the product life cycles in information technology this is a remarkable achievement. Figure 4.8 shows one of the few Z-Wave products of the first generation, developed in the early 2000s. It's not longer in production but the device will work well even in modern networks and can be controlled by any Z-Wave controller that was ever designed.

However, compatibility is only a one-way street. It's impossible to develop products that will be **compatible to functions** that**will be invented in the future**. This does not forbid interoperability and compatibility but may be perceived as such.

**Example:**

A remote control developed in 2007 is able to switch switches, dimm dimmers and control motors to move blinds or doors. It was certified and works well. In 2009/2010, time frame a new category of lighting devices becomes available - multi color LEDs. Multi color LEDs can adapt the temperature of the light to the user needs or can be turned into almost any color imaginable.

The Z-Wave alliance has reacted to this new product category and has specified a way how Z-Wave controller can define the color of a multi-color LED. This command class `Color Control Command Class` was finalized in 2010 and right after finalizing the first products using this technology are hitting the streets.

The multi-color-LEDs are backward compatible. They can still be switched and dimmed the way a light was switched or dimmed before. A user can use his old remote control to dim and switch the LED but he can not choose the LEDs light color by this remote control because this color picking function did not exist when the remote control was developed.

Users may perceive this as incompatibility.

## 4.3.4. Multi Channels versus Multi Instances

There is no rule without exception and while Z-Wave maintains backward compatibility at no compromise, the exception is called `Multi Instance Command Class`. Here is the story:

Initially it was assumed that every device only has one function of its kind. A switch device has one relay, a dimmer device has one dimmer. Later on it became obvious that it makes much sense to have similar functions in one device. A good example would be a power strip where all the outlets shall be switches. The power strip shall be controlled by one single Z-Wave transceiver but the `Switch Binary` command class does not support multiple switching functions.

In order to maintain backward compatibily of all devices supporting and controlling binary switches another command class was introduced that allows to differentiate multiple instances of a device. This device class was called `Multi Instance Command Class`.

After the introduction of this command class it turned out that the command creates more problems than it solved and quickly a second version of the command class was developed. To differentiate from the first version it was called `Multi Channel Command Class`. For some intermediate time devices with the `Multi Instance Command Class` were still accepted in certification but meanwhile the command class is really abandoned and must not be used anymore. Fortunately, only very few devices were ever introduced using the old `Multi Instance Command Class`, among them however a lot of devices from the German manufacturer Merten, now part of Schneider Elektrik.

As a result there are quite a few incompatibilities between `Multi Instance Command Class` products and all other Z-Wave products. Very few gateways - like Z-Way from Z-wave.me[Z-Wave.Me] - support both `Multi Instance Command Class` and `Multi Channel Command Class` but the majority just ignores the old `Multi Instance Command Class`.

Together with the introduction of the `Multi Channel Command Class` a new command class for handling associations with these devices was needed. The `Multi Channel Association Command Class` extends the normal Association command class to allow to set different instances of a device into an association group.

## 4.3.5. Sins from the past

When Z-Wave was introduced to the market in the early 2000s, the certification was less strict so that devices were certified that would not get a certification granted anymore. These old devices may create problems because they simply don't follow the standard in all aspects. Fortunately, these products more and more disappear. However, some of them may still be around. Appenix C points to an online ressource of a black list of products that fall into this category. The vast majority of these products are in the list because of missing support of `Multi Channel Association Command Class` as just explained above.

## 4.3.6. IP Gateways

Smart homes are at the intersection of two different worlds. On the one hand there is the conservative world of facility management, house installation and installers. They don't have the intention to 'play' with products for too long. Their technology is stable and well proven.

On the other hand there is the information technology and here namely the software business. Here we see frequent product updates, software patches and release changes.

IP gateways certainly belong into the group of IT equipment. Frequent software updates, feature enhancements, bug fixes etc. cause a constant change if the user wants to follow all the updates. It's not uncommon that a firmware for an IP gateway gets released just followed by another one after few days fixing a bug that was just introduced in the first place.

## 4.3.7. Weak Check Sum

Chapter 2.6.5 describes the Checksum algorithm used in Z-Wave and discussed the weakness of the legacy solution. Particularly for data collection and large messages the weak checksum results in wrong transmissions from time to time. Z-Wave has therefore introduced a new system that protects metering data with another 17 bit strong check sum. In order to use this new strong protection of data both the device and the controller need to support it.

# 5. Special topics around Z-Wave

## 5.1. Legal situation

The Z-Wave communication architecture consists of various parts that have different legal status.

Figure 5.1 gives an overview of the different parts of Z-Wave.

- PHY: The physical layer that deals with frequencies, framing, error detection etc. is specified by the ITU-T under G.9959 and therefore public domain.

- PHY: The media access layer that deals with Node IDs, Home IDs, addresses, retransmission etc. is specified by the ITU-T under G.9959 and therefore public domain.

- NET: The network layer that deals with Inclusion, Routing and Network reorganization remains intellectual property of Sigma Designs and is offered royalty-free to all manufacturers that want to develop and manufacture Z-Wave devices.

- APP: The application layer that defines what a product is doing and how it is acting is owned by the man-

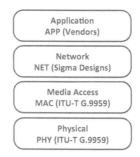

Figure 5.1.: Different Layers of Z-Wave

ufacturer of the device. However, the implementation of this layer must use the device class and command class specification provided by the Z-Wave Alliance resp. Sigma Designs.

The ITU-T specification G.9959 is freely available and all implementations of the protocol are free of patent claims or any other royalty payment needs. Figure 5.2 shows the cover page of the official ITU-T spec.

## 5.1.1. Important Patents of Z-Wave

The networking layer of Z-Wave is protected among others by the following patents, all held by Sigma Designs:

- US6856236: *RF home automation system comprising nodes with dual functionality, filed April 25th, 2001* A system that has multiple devices with receiver, transmitter, a CPU and memory to store identifiers; a con-

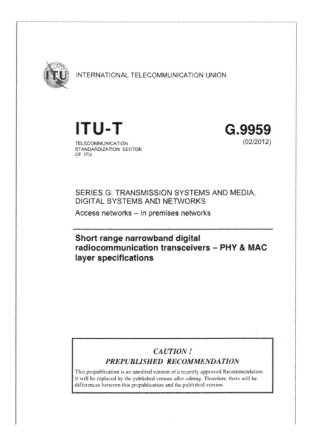

Figure 5.2.: Cover Page of ITU-T G.9959

troller with receiver, transmitter, memory to store the identifiers of the devices and another memory to hold the controllers own identifier information, and a processor one or more devices that can act as repeaters by receiving information, processing them and sending them out again and one or more devices that act as I/O devices, means generating an event signal in response to received input.

- US6879806: *System and a method of building routing tables and for routing signals in an automation system, filed June 1st, 2001* A system defined in US6856236 that is able to build neighborhood tables that can be used for routing.

- US6980080: *RF home automation system with replicable controllers, filed April 25, 2001* A system defined in US6856236 that allows transferring routing information from one controller to another controller.

- US7680041: *Node Repair in a mesh network, files Mar, 9th, 2007* The use of SUC and SIS in a meshed network.

## 5.1.2. Important Patents challenging Z-Wave

The Z-Wave core definitions are not subject to any patent dispute. However, real implementations of Z-Wave networks use certain architectures or processes that are covered by third parties patents. This has led to certain patent ligitations and licensing agreements of Z-Wave manufacturers.

**The Lutron Patent**

The US company Lutron has filed the patent 5.905.442 in the mid nineties describing the wireless control of lights from wall switches. The patent relates specifically to wireless networks with mesh routing functions. That's why a lot of the simpler wireless technologies on the market do not infringe the patent but Z-Wave does. The key patent claim No 1 describes: *1. Apparatus for controlling at least one electrical device by remote control comprising: at least one control device coupled to the electrical device by a wire connection for providing power to the electrical device, the control device having a controllably conductive device for adjusting the status of said electrical device, the control device further having a manual actuator for adjusting the status of the electrical device, the control device further having a radio frequency transmitter/receiver and antenna coupled thereto for adjusting the status of the electrical device in response to control information in a radio frequency signal, the transmitter/receiver being coupled to the antenna of the control device for receiving the radio frequency signal and for transmitting a status radio frequency signal having status information therein regarding the status of the electrical device as affected by the control information and the manual actuator; a master control unit having at least one actuator and status indicator thereon, the master unit comprising a transmitter/receiver for transmitting a radio frequency signal having the control information therein to control the status of said at least one electrical device and for receiving the status information from the control device, the status indicator indicating the status of the electrical device in response to the status information; and a repeater transmitter/receiver for receiving the radio frequency signal from the master unit and transmitting the control information to the control device and for receiving the status information from the control device and transmitting the status information to the master unit.*

Every sending of a status signal as result of a local status change of a wireless device in a routed network infringes this patent. This is the reason why manufacturers of Z-Wave device intentionally did not implement a status report function as a result of local status change.

As a result the gateway does not recognize a local status change of the device and will remain showing a wrong status of this particular device.

Meanwhile people found - as almost always - a way to solve the problem without infringing the Lutron Patent. Devices such as wall switches, wall dimmers or outlet plug switches and dimmers with a local button offer an association group to operate remote devicessimultaneously to the loca loperation. Using the local button is not only switching the local state but is causing to send a switching command to an association group. The main difference to the patent-protected scenario is that there is no longer a status report (protected by patent) but a switching command (allowed by the patent). Beside other switches, that can be switched simultaneously with the particular button on one switch the gateway itself may also be a target device. In this case the gateway must emulate the behaviour of a standard switch to be able to receive switching commands. Receiving a switching command from a wall switch will not cause the gateway to switch on a lamp but to immediately check the status of this particular switch and, subsequently, update the switch state on the gateways GUI. One other method is to just send a Hail command that may be used to poll the device status.

## The Sipco Patents

Sipco is a very small US company that has filed certain inventions around the use of mesh networking back in the year of 2000. Although these systems were never manufactured or sold the description and patents around these ideas provide very valuable intellectual property to the inventor.

The main patents hold by SIPCO and used against Z-Wave device manufacturers are:

- US6891838: System and Method for monitoring and controlling residential devices

- US6914893: System and Method for monitoring and controlling remote devices

- US7103511: Wireless Communication Networks for providing remote monitoring of devices

The claims of these patents are focused ro the access of a meshed short range wireless network via a gateway to the internet. This means that all manufacturers of IP gateways or their customers are subject to a possible violation of this patent.

All patents mentioned in the sections above are valid in the USA only. There is no such patent problems known in Europe.

## 5.2. SDKs

All Z-Wave devices run a firmware that consists of two parts: There is a fixed part delivered by Sigma Designs that covers all network related functions and there is a vendor specific part, that the vendors define and implement according to the Z-Wave specification. The part provided by Sigma is called **Systems Development Kit (SDK)** and has different release numbers. Certain versions of this SDK introduced new functions. These SDKs are always backward compatible but the new functions are then available only for this SDK and subsequent SDK numbers. The following SDKs were released:

- SDK 3.0x: First Generation of Z-Wave chip ZW0102

- SDK 3.20: introduces Static Update Controller (SUC) in 2003

- SDK 3.40: SUC ID Server (SIS) in 2005

- SDK 4.00: Second Generation of Z-Wave chip ZW0201 in 2005

- SDK 4.20: Silent Acknowledge in 2006

- SDK 5.0x: Third Generation of Z-Wave chip ZW0301 in 2007

- SDK 4.5x: Explorer Frame plus Network Wide Inclusion in 2009

- SDK 6.0x: Fourth Generation of Z-Wave chip ZW0401 in 2010

- SDK 6.5x: Fifth Generation of Z-Wave chip (series 500) in 2013

All SDKs before 3.40 can be considered as obsolete and only very few products are still in the market based on these SDKs. All SDKs from 4.20 but not 4.5x and the SDK 5.x typically all referred to as SDK 5 share the same support for the basic Z-Wave network functions and processes, namely the SUC/SIS support. The SDKs 4.5x plus all SDKs from 6.x add explorer frame support that greatly enhance the way the network is self reorganizing in case of changes. All products based on these SDKs are 100 % backward compatible to the older SDKs.

Figure 5.3 shows how a Z-Wave software indicates the SDK version used for the Z-Wave transceiver chip.

## 5.3. General Info about Dimmers

Dimmers are electrical devices. They allow to continuously dimm a light according to the users requirement. There are multiple types of electrical lights and unfortunately there is no dimmer able to dim all lights.

Lamps can be

- The classical incandescent light invented by Thomas Alva Edison

- Halogen lamps operated by 230 V AC (High Voltage Halogen)

- Halogen lamps operated by 24 V (Low Voltage Halogen). The conversion from 230 V down to 24 V is done

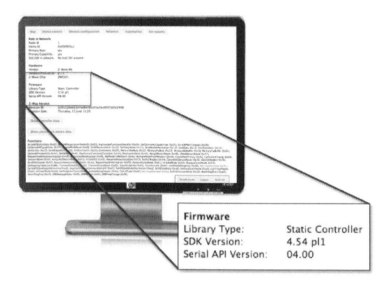

Figure 5.3.: SDK Version shown in Z-Way Software

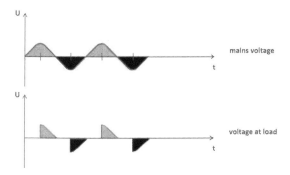

Figure 5.4.: Voltage at leading-edge phase control dimmer

in two different ways: (a) using a simple transformer or (b) using an electronic switching power supply.

- Fluorescent Light in general, and compact fluorescent light (CFL) in particular. They are also called energy saving lamps.

- Lamps based on Light Emitting Diodes, called LED lights

## 5.3.1. Leading-edge phase control

Conventional lamps are dimmed using a so-called leading edge phase control. This means that a changing portion of the sine wave is cut off. The resulting energy is reduced and the light is dimmed. Figure 5.4 shows a sine wave for full load and for 50

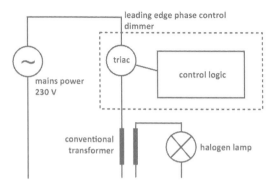

Figure 5.5.: Schematics of a leading edge phase control dimmer

At leading edge dimmers the Voltage remains 0 after the wave crossed the zero line. After the defined time a Triac is ignited. This brings the full voltage of the sine wave to the lamp. The characteristic of a Triac is to block the current again when the sine wave crosses the zero line. Hence, the Triac needs to be ignited at every current wave again.

Leading Edge Dimmers work well with incandescent lights and HV Halogen light but fail to dim low voltage Halogen, Fluorescent lamps and LED lamps. Even worse, they may even destroy these lamps.

## 5.3.2. Leading Edge Phase Control for inductive loads

Transformers used in Low Voltage Halogen Lamps realize an inductive load. A load is called predominantly inductive

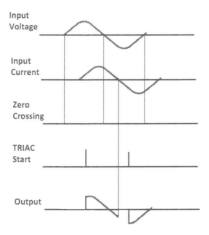

Figure 5.6.: Current Shift on inductive loads result in dis-
balanced waveform

if the alternating load current lags behind the alternating
voltage of the load. Such a load is also known as lagging
load. This means that the voltage is already at zero while
the current is not zero yet.

This creates a huge problem for traditional cutting edge
dimmers using a Triac. The Triac closes when the current
is zero, not when the voltage is zero. This may result in
a waveform that does not have symmetric waves for the
negative and the positive wave part as shown in Figure 5.6.
This however results in a DC current part of the output that
may destroy a transformer connected as load.

To dim halogen lamps with conventional transformers a
special electronic is needed to make sure that the Triac

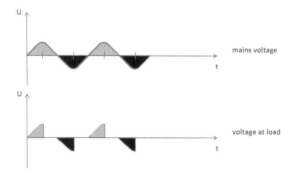

Figure 5.7.: Voltage at a trailing edge phase control dimmer

switches at the right time. These dimmers can still dim all conventional - resistive - loads

## 5.3.3. Trailing Edge Phase Control Dimmer

Electronic Power supplies typically represent a conductive load. In a conductive load the capacitive reactance exceeds the inductive reactance. Hence the load draws a leading current. To dim these loads a trailing edge phase control dimmer is needed.

The trailing edge dimmer cuts off the trailing part of the sine wave like shown in Figure 5.7. Such behaviour cannot be achieved using a Triac component. High Voltage MOS-FET components are used instead.

Figure 5.8 shows the schematics of such a dimmer.

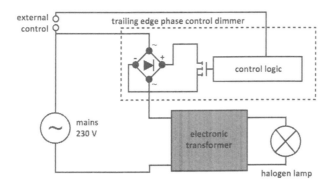

Figure 5.8.: Schematics of a trailing edge phase control dimmer

## 5.3.4. Universal Dimmers

The dilemma of edge phase control dimmers is that - in case of leading edge either inductive loads or - in case of reactive loads- capacitive loads can be dimmed. The dimmer may even destroy the load not supported.

The solution is a so-called universal dimmer.

Universal dimmers detect initially if the load has inductive or reactive characteristics and change between leading and trailing edge. To make sure the detection delivers the correct result, the user needs to make sure that only one load is connected to the dimmer during power on. Also changing the load later on may result in problems. The biggest challenge of universal dimmers however is the higher price point compared to normal leadign edge dimmers.

## 5.3.5. Fluorescent Lamps

Conventional Fluorescent Lights are not dimmable. However, there are special transformer devices capable to dim of these devices. For CFLs these transformers are already integrated in the lamp socket. CFLs with this unit are called dimmable CFLs and usually have a much higher price.

CFL are typically dimmed either by a trailing edge dimmer or a universal dimmer. Manufacturers of modern CFLs have done a good job in compensating the reactive load, so that even normal leading edge dimmers can dim such a lamp.

## 5.3.6. LED Lamps

LED lamps can be dimmed very well but neither with leading nor with training edge dimmers. There are dimmers using a so-called PWM (pulse wide modulation). Hence LED lights need a special dimmer only applicable for LED lights.

## 5.3.7. Dimmer Summary

Table 5.1 gives a summary overview of the different types of dimmers and the types of lamps dimmable.

| Phases | Leading edge | Leading edge with inductive support | Trailing edge | Universal |
|---|---|---|---|---|
| Electric light bulb | Yes | Yes | Yes | Yes |
| HV Halogen | Yes | Yes | Yes | Yes |
| Low Voltage Halogen (conv. Transformer) | No | Yes | No | Yes |
| Low Voltage Halogen (Switched power supply) | No | No | Yes | Yes |
| Dimmable Fluorescent lamp | No | Yes | No | Yes |
| LED lamp | No | No | No | No |

Table 5.1.: Conditions to change state for battery operated devices

# A. Device Classes in Z-Wave

- Alarm Sensor Generic Device Class
  - No Specific Device Class defined
  - Basic Routing Alarm Sensor Specific Device Class
  - Routing Alarm Sensor Specific Device Class
  - Basic Zensor Net Alarm Sensor Specific Device Class
  - Zensor Net Alarm Sensor Specific Device Class
  - Advanced Zensor Net Alarm Sensor Specific Device Class
  - Basic Routing Smoke Sensor Specific Device Class
  - Routing Smoke Sensor Specific Device Class
  - Basic Zensor Net Smoke Sensor Specific Device Class
  - Zensor Net Smoke Sensor Specific Device Class
  - Advanced Zensor Net Smoke Sensor Specific Device Class.

- Binary Switch Generic Device Class
  - No Specific Device Class defined

## A. Device Classes in Z-Wave

  - – Binary Power Switch Specific Device Class
  - – Binary Scene Switch Specific Device Class

- Remote Controller Generic Device Class
  - – Portable Remote Controller Specific Device Class
  - – Portable Scene Controller Specific Device Class
  - – Portable Installer Tool Specific Device Class

- Static Controller Generic Device Class
  - – PC Controller Specific Device Class
  - – Scene Controller Specific Device Class
  - – Static Installer Tool Specific Device Class

- Repeater Slave Generic Device Class Basic
  - – Repeater Slave Specific Device

- Multilevel Switch Generic Device Class
  - – No Specific Device Class defined
  - – Multilevel Power Switch Specific Device Class
  - – Multilevel Scene Switch Specific Device Class
  - – Multiposition Motor Specific Device Class (Not recommended)
  - – Motor Control Class A Specific Device Class
  - – Motor Control Class B Specific Device Class
  - – Motor Control Class C Specific Device Class

- Remote Switch Generic Device Class
  - – Binary Remote Switch Specific Device Class

- Multilevel Remote Switch Specific Device Class
- Binary Sensor Generic Device Class
  - Routing Binary Sensor Specific Device Class
- Multilevel Sensor Generic Device Class
  - Routing Multilevel Sensor Specific Device Class
- Pulse Meter Generic Device Class
- Display Generic Device Class
  - No Specific Device Class defined
  - Simple Display Specific Device Class
- Entry Control Generic Device Class
  - Specific Device Class Not Used
  - Door Lock Specific Device Class
  - Advanced Door Lock Specific Device Class
  - Secure Keypad Door Lock Specific Device Class
- Semi Interoperable Generic Device Class
  - Energy Production Specific Device Class
- Thermostat Generic Device Class
  - Thermostat General V2 Specific Device Class
  - Setback Schedule Thermostat Specific Device Class
  - Setback Thermostat Specific Device
  - Setpoint Thermostat Specific Device Class
- AV Control Point Generic Device Class

## A. Device Classes in Z-Wave

   - No Specific Device Class defined
   - Satellite Receiver V2 Specific Device Class
   - Doorbell Specific Device Class

- Meter Generic Device Class
  - No Specific Device Class defined
  - Simple Meter Specific Device Class

- Ventilation Generic Device Class
  - No Specific Device Class defined
  - Residential Heat Recovery Ventilation Specific Device Class

- Z/IP Gateway Generic Device Class
  - Z/IP Tunneling Gateway Specific Device Class
  - Advanced Z/IP Gateway Specific Device Class

- Z/IP Node Generic Device Class
  - Z/IP Tunneling Node Specific Device
  - Advanced Z/IP Node Specific Device Class

# B. Command Classes in Z-Wave

This gives you an overview of the the most important command classes of Z-Wave including the user revelant commands. There may be more commands defined in the respective command class, but they are used for internal maintenance of the command class, e.g. during the interview process. [1]

**0x71: Alarm - handles alarm conditions**  Commands to Node

- Get(type, ztype)

- Set(type)

- Unset(type)

Commands to Node

- alarmReport()

---

[1]The syntax of the user relevant calls are taken from the python implementation of Z-Way. For more information on Z-Way please refer to http://www.zwave.me

## B. *Command Classes in Z-Wave*

**0x9C: AlarmSensor - reads Alarm sensor data**  Commands to Node

- Get(type)

Commands to Node

- sensorAlarmReport()

**0x9D: AlarmSilence - turns on/off alarm conditions**  Commands to Node

- Set(mode, sec, mask)

**0x22: ApplicationStatus: allowsto delay communication is node is busy**  Commands from Node

- applicationBusy()

- applicationRejectedRequest()

**0x85: Association - manages association groups**  Commands to Node

- Get(groupId)

- Set(groupId, includeNode)

- Remove(groupId, excludeNode)

- GroupingsGet()

Commands to Node

- associationSet()

- associationRemove()

- associationReport()

## 0x9b: AssociationCommandConfiguration - defines node individual commands in association groups  Commands to Node

- Get(groupId, nodeId)

- Set(groupId, nodeId, cmd)

Commands to Node

- commandConfigurationReport()

## 0x20: Basic - generic control class with node-individual interpretation of commands  Commands to Node

- Get()

- Set(value)

Commands to Node

- Report()

## 0x80: Battery - reports battery charging status  Commands to Node

- Get()

Commands to Node

- Report()

## 0x46: ClimateControlSchedule - defines a whole weekly schedule for a climate control device   Commands to Node

- Get(,weekday)

- OverrideGet()

- OverrideSet(state, type)

- Set(weekday, points)

Commands to Node

- schedulGet()

- scheduleChangedGet()

- scheduleOverrideGet()

- scheduleOverrideReport()

## 0x81: Clock - handles clock data   Commands to Node

- Get()

- Set()

Commands to Node

- Report()

**0x70: Configuration - sets device specific configuration parameters** Commands to Node

- Get(parameter)

- SetDefault(parameter)

- BulkSet(parameterlist)

- Set(parameter, value)

Commands to Node

- Report()

- BulkReport()

**0x62: DoorLock - operates door locks** Commands to Node

- Set(mode)

- ConfigurationSet(opType, outsideState, insideState, lockMin, lockSec)

- Get()

- ConfigurationGet()

Commands to Node

- operationReport()

- configurationReport()

## B. Command Classes in Z-Wave

### 0x4C: DoorLockLogging - access too door lock logging
Commands to Node

- Get(record)

Commands to Node

- loggingRecordsSupportedReport()

- Report()

### 0x7A: FirmwareUpdateMD - firmware update over the air   Commands to Node

- Get()

- RequestUpdate(url, firmwareId, vendorId)

Commands to Node

- Report()

- requestReport()

- mdGet()

- mdStatusReport()

### 0x82: Hail - just say Hi   Commands to Node

- Hail()

## 0x87: Indicator - handles behavior of local indicator on device (e.g. LED) Commands to Node

- Get()
- Set(,val)

Commands to Node

- Report()

## 0x72: ManufacturerSpecific - identifies the product Commands to Node

- Get()

Commands from Node

- Report()

## 0x32: Meter - handles meters and meter data Commands to Node

- Get(scale)
- Reset()

Commands to Node

- Report()

## 0x35: MeterPulse - handles pulse meters Commands to Node

- Get()

Commands to Node

- Report()

**0x3D: MeterTableMonitor - reads out meter history**  Commands to Node

- GetCurrentData()

- GetHistoricalData(start, stop, reports)

- GetStatusDepth(depth)

- GetStatusData(start, stop, reports)

Commands to Node

- statusSupportedReport:()

- tablePointAdmNoReport()

- tableIdReport()

- Report:()

**0x60: MultiChannel - handles multiple similar functions within one device**  Commands to Node

- Get(ccId)

- EndpointFind(generic, specific)

- ChannelEndpointGet()

- ChannelCapabilitiesGet(endPoint)

- Encapsulate(data, endpoint)

Commands to Node

- Report()

## 0x8E: MultiChannelAssociation - handles association in case of Multi channel devices   Commands to Node

- Get(groupId)

- Set(groupId, includeNode, includeInstance)

- Remove(groupId, excludeNode, excludeInstance)

- GroupingsGet()

Commands to Node

- Report()

## 0x8F: MultiCmd - wrapper for multiple commands in one frame   Commands to Node

- Encapsulate(data[])

Commands to Node

- enCap()

## 0x77: NodeNaming - allows to set names to individual devices   Commands to Node

- Get()

- GetName()

- GetLocation()

- SetName(name)

- SetLocation(name)

## B. Command Classes in Z-Wave

Commands to Node

- nodeNameReport()

- nodeLocationReport()

### 0x00: NoOperation   Commands to Node

- SendNoOperation()

### 0x73: PowerLevel - controls the transmitter power level
Commands to Node

- Get()

- TestToNode(nodeid)

- Set(level, timeout)

Commands to Node

- Report()

- testNodeReport()

### 0x75: Protection - handles child protection of local operation   Commands to Node

- Get()

- ExclusiveGet()

- ExclusiveSet(nodeid)

- TimeoutGet()

- TimeoutSet(timeout)

- Set(state, rfState )

Commands to Node

- Report()

- timeoutReport()

**0x2B: SceneActivation - command to activate a scene**
Commands to Node

- Set(sceneId, dimmingDuration)

**0x2C: SceneActuatorConf - define behavior in actor when scene activation command is received** Commands to Node

- Get(scene)

- Set(scene, level, dimming, override)

Commands to Node

- Report()

**0x2D: SceneControllerConf - defines the relationship between association group and scene ID** Commands to Node

- Get(group)

- Set(group, scene, duration)

Commands to Node

- Report()

**0x4E: ScheduleEntryLock - defines times when a door lock is active**   Commands to Node

- Set(user, status)

- AllSet(status)

- WeekDayScheduleSet(user)

- WeekDayScheduleDelete(user)

- YearScheduleSet(user, status)

- WeekDayScheduleGet(user, slot)

- YearScheduleGet(user, slot)

Commands to Node

- Report()

- yearDayReport()

- weekDayReport()

**0x98: Security - wrapper for secure communication**   Commands to Node

- Encrypt(data, key)

Commands to Node

- securityMessageEncapsulation()

**0x30: SensorBinary - handles binary sensors**  Commands to Node

- Get()

Commands to Node

- Report()

**0x9E: SensorConfiguration - specific configuration of sensors, particularly trigger levels**  Commands to Node

- Get()
- Set(mode, value)

Commands to Node

- triggerLevelReport()

**0x31: SensorMultilevel - handles multilevel sensors**  Commands to Node

- Get()

Commands to Node

- Report()

**0x94: SimpleAVControl - handles behavior or Audio/Video Remote Controls**  Commands to Node

- Set(mediaItem, *buttons)
- Get()

Commands to Node

- simpleAvControlReport()

**0x27: SwitchAll - defines behavior on `switch all` command** Commands to Node

- Get()

- SetOn()

- SetOff()

- Set(mode)

Commands to Node

- Report()

**0x25: SwitchBinary - handles binary switch** Commands to Node

- Get()

- Set(value)

Commands to Node

- Report()

**0x26: SwitchMultilevel - handles multilevel switch** Commands to Node

- Get()

- Set(level, duration)

- SetWithDuration(level, duration)

- StartLevelChange(dir, duration = 0xff, ignoreStartLevel, startLevel)

- StartLevelChangeWithDuration(dir, duration, ignoreStartLevel)

- StopLevelChange()

Commands to Node

- Report()

## 0x44: ThermostatFanMode - controls Thermostat Fan Modes   Commands to Node

- Get()

- Set(mode)

Commands to Node

- Report()

## 0x40: ThermostatMode controls Thermostat Modes   Commands to Node

- Get()

- Set(mode)

Commands to Node

- Report()

## 0x43: ThermostatSetPoint - defines the set point of thermostats in different modes   Commands to Node

- Get(mode)

- Set(mode, value)

Commands to Node

- Report()

## 0x8A: Time - handles timing information   Commands to Node

- TimeGet()

- OffsetGet()

- DateGet()

- TimeOffsetSet()

Commands to Node

- timeReport()

- dateReport()

## 0x8B: TimeParameters - handles timing parameters   Commands to Node

- Get()

- Set()

Commands to Node

- Report()

## 0x63: UserCode - defines user access codes for door locks    Commands to Node

- Get(user )
- Set(user, code)

Commands to Node

- Report()
- numberReport()

## 0x86: Version - reports version of device an versions of other command classes    Commands to Node

- Get()
- CommandClassVersionGet(ccId)

Commands to Node

- commandclassReport()
- Report()

## 0x84: Wakeup - handles periodical wakeup of battery-operated devices    Commands to Node

- Get()
- Set(interval, notificationNodeId)
- Sleep()

Commands to Node

- intervalReport()
- wakeupNotification()

# C. Useful Online Ressources

There are plenty of online ressources about Z-Wave. Just google for Z-Wave or check out Youtube or other media services for content in regard to Z-Wave. Here are some selected web sites with useful Z-Wave related content.

**http://www.z-wavealliance.org**  This is the central page for all Z-Wave Alliance members including member section, newsletter management, etc

**http://www.zwaveproducts.com**  One of the leading online stores for US Z-Wave products

**http://www.zwave4u.com**  One of the leading online stores for Euroean Z-Wave products

**http://www.zwave.com**  The end user facing page of Z-Wave

**http://www.zwaveurope.com**  Homepage of the European Master distributor of Z-Wave

## C. Useful Online Ressources

**http://wiki.zwaveurope.com**  Nice collection of technical background papers and HowTo, focused on European Devices

**http://pepper1.net/zwavedb/**  An online database of Z-Wave products with comprehensive technical data

**http://www.z-wave.me**  A free cloud service running Z-Way, a certified Z-Wave controller software

**http://code.google.com/p/open-zwave/**  An open source project implementing the Z-Wave protocol

# Bibliography

[SmartHome] http://en.wikipedia.org/wiki/Smarthome

[6LoPAN] http://en.wikipedia.org/wiki/6LoWPAN

[Merten2007] http://www.merten.com/

[CEPT] http://www.cept.org/

[Merten2008] Merten CONNECT Product Literature

[Z-Way2012] Z-Wave.Me: *Z-Way Users and Installation Manual*, 2012

[Sigma2008] Press Release Sigma Designs Dec, 18th, 2008: *Sigma Designs Acquires Zensys* http://www.silicontap.com/sigma_designs_acquires_zensys/s-0019088.html

[Mitsumi2011] Mitsumi Electric Co, Ltd Press Release : *Mitsumi concluded Z-Wave Module Supply Agreement with Sigma Designs, Inc. in USA* , May23rd, 2011, http://www.mitsumi.co.jp/pdf/20110523_e.pdf

[ITU2012] ITU-T G.9959: *Short range narrowband digital radiocommunication transceivers - PHY & MAC layer specification*, International Telecommunication Union, 02/2012

# Bibliography

[Sigma300] Sigma Designs, Ltd *ZM3102 Z-Wave Module, Data Sheet* , October, 2007, http://media.digikey.com/pdf/_Data%20Sheets /Zensys_%20PDFs/ZM3102N.pdf

[Z-Wave.Me] Homepage: www.zwave.me

[Seluxit] Homeepage: www.seluxit.com

[ZSTICK] http://www.zwaveeurope.com

[OpenZWave] Open Source Z-Wave Implementation in C, code.google.com/p/open-zwave/

[PepperOne] Homepage: www.pepper-one.de

[Bulogics] Homepage: www.bulogics.com/

[KEIL] Homepage: www.keil.com/

# List of Tables

## List of Tables

# List of Figures

# Index

Made in the USA
Lexington, KY
26 August 2013